46 Leatherwork Projects

ANYONE CAN DO

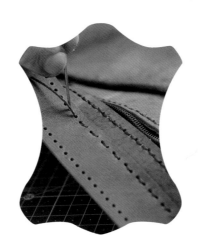

STACKPOLE
BOOKS
Guilford, Connecticut

46 Leatherwork Projects

Anyone Can Do

GEERT SCHUILING

Woodheads
1867

Published by Stackpole Books
An imprint of Globe Pequot
www.rowman.com

Distributed by National Book Network
800-462-6420

First Stackpole Books paperback edition, 2017

Originally published in 2016 by
Metz Press
1 Cameronians Avenue
Welgemoed, 7530 South Africa

Publisher: Wilsia Metz
Photographer: Ivan Naudé
Text: Monean Winterbach
Templates: Alan Cuba
Designer: Liezl Maree
Proofreader: Nikki Metz
Printed and bound in China by
    1010 Printing International Ltd

British Library Cataloguing in Publication
Information Available

Library of Congress Cataloging-in-Publication
Data Available

ISBN: 978-0-8117-1996-4

Contents

Acknowledgments

First of all I would like to thank my wife Rachel, my daughters Marijke, Laura, and Emily, and my son Jannes, who have always encouraged me to pursue the idea of making leather craft easy and accessible to young and old.

I also thank Richard Harris, owner of Woodheads, who has made it possible to put this book together here at Woodheads with my colleagues Enoch Mqwebedu, a master leather crafter, and Alan Cuba, who put together all the scale drawings.

Thank you Wilsia Metz, for enthusiastically wanting to add this leather craft book to the range of craft books published by Metz Press.

A big thank you to Monean Winterbach, who sat with me writing everything into a readable format, and Ivan Naudé of Planet Ivan for the beautiful photographs.

Finally, a special thank you to all the leather crafters, designers, and colleagues over the years who have inspired me with their ideas and support.

INTRODUCTION

This book is about easy-to-do leather craft—from simple to make to more advanced, everyday leather items. The idea is to show you how you can make these items with basic techniques, tools, and supplies. All the patterns are provided to scale from which you can make your templates.

Two types of leather are used for these projects—natural vegetable-tanned leather and chrome-tanned leather such as upholstery leather, side leather, and suede.

The items are all plain, but you can embellish them with a variety of techniques such as painting, carving, embossing, beadwork, lacing, embroidery, etc.

All the projects in the book are items that are constantly requested from Woodheads—our most popular products. The patterns have been customized for hand-stitching to accommodate the widest range of crafters.

I hope you enjoy making these leather items and whenever you are in Cape Town, come say hello at Woodheads and share your masterpieces with us!

Warm regards,

Geert Schuiling

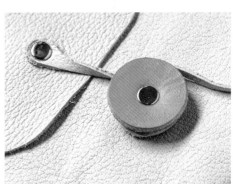

Tools and their uses

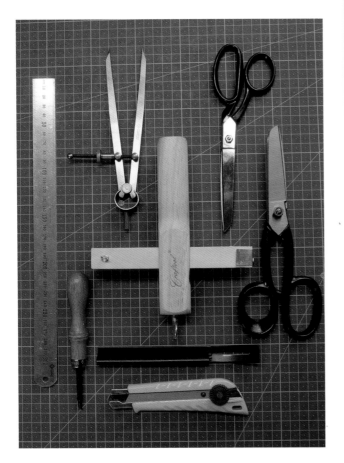

Cutting mat

Use a self-healing cutting mat to work on; this will protect your work surface. They come in various sizes.

NT cutter

This cutting knife is generally used to cut leather freehand or along a metal ruler. The NT cutter can also be used instead of a skiving knife to skive off the ends of leather parts to reduce the thickness when layering two pieces of leather on top of each other.

Leather scissors

Leather scissors are not the same as fabric scissors. One blade is serrated, which prevents the leather from slipping when you are cutting it.

Revolving punch pliers (assorted hole sizes)

Revolving punch pliers are used to hand-punch holes into leather. The trick with using revolving punch pliers is to press down and twist the tool while punching, performing a drilling action.

Junior punch pliers

These have a single punch mainly used for punching stitching holes into the leather.

MINI OR MAXI ROUND-HOLE PUNCH SET (ASSORTED HOLE SIZES)

This tool is used to punch holes into leather where the revolving punch pliers or the junior punch pliers cannot reach, or where more force is needed to punch the hole. To use these punches, you need a nylon pad and nylon mallet. The leather is placed on the nylon pad and the punch is positioned over the hole marking. Ensure that the tool is held completely upright (vertical). Hit down on the punch with the nylon mallet to punch the hole. Never use a steel hammer as it will damage your tools.

HOLLOW SLOT PUNCH (ASSORTED SIZES)

This punch is used on belts or straps to create the slot for the buckle prong and the slots to use when threading straps through leather. It is used in the same way as the mini or maxi round-hole punch set.

NYLON MALLET AND NYLON PAD

A nylon mallet is used with hollow punches and other similar tools to hit down on the tool to punch the hole. The nylon mallet will not damage the tools. It is always used in conjunction with a nylon pad (the leather is placed on the nylon pad).

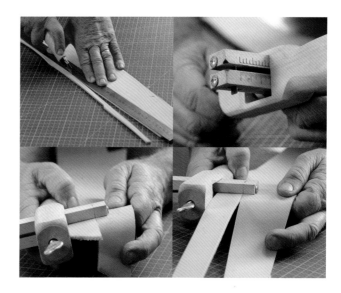

STRAP CUTTER

The strap cutter enables you to accurately cut strips and straps needed in leather projects such as belts and handbag slings. Follow the manufacturer's instructions carefully to ensure that you cut the correct width and length. Make sure that your leather has a straight edge before you start cutting.

STEEL HAMMER

There are instances where a steel hammer is needed instead of the nylon mallet. When attaching a buckle using rivets, the steel hammer comes in handy. It can also be used to shape leather or secure glued leather pieces together.

RUBBER MALLET

The rubber mallet is used to firm down glued surfaces or soles of sandals and shoes without marking these surfaces.

BELT TIP AND END PUNCHES

Belt tip and end punches are used to neatly shape the tips and ends of leather belts and straps. They come in point and half-round shapes and are used with the nylon mallet and pad.

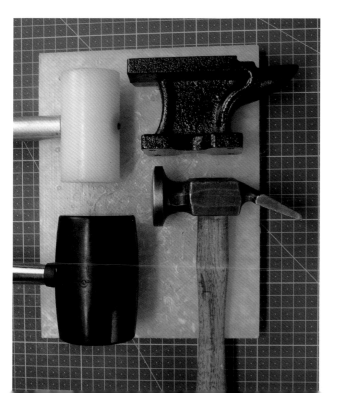

Needles

HARNESS NEEDLE

These are used when hand-stitching leather with waxed braided thread. The harness needle has a blunt tip; it is used to stitch through prepunched holes, therefore a sharp tip is not required.

SAIL NEEDLE

This needle has a sharp tip and is used when you need to stitch through an additional layer, such as a zipper, without prepunched holes.

TIP: When stitching a zipper to leather inserting the needle from the back (zipper side), insert it from the punched hole in the front first to prick through the zipper tape, then insert the needle from the back where you've pricked the tape.

Metal anvil

This is used as the firm base when securing press studs, rivets, eyelets, and so on with a steel hammer.

Scratch awl

The scratch awl is used when marking leather (holes and cutting lines) as well as to scratch (roughen) the surface of the leather before gluing pieces together.

Dividers

Dividers have many uses in leather craft.
- Use them as compasses to draw circles with a center point.
- Crease a line on the edge of the leather, parallel with the edge, for decorative purposes or a stitch line.
- Divide the circumference of a leather panel into evenly spaced measurements and mark evenly spaced punch holes by pricking.

Rivet setter

A rivet setter is used to secure a rivet when you want to keep the dome shape of the cap. Using a hammer as an alternative will flatten the cap to create a flat surface. See instructions on page 22.

Press-stud tool

The press-stud tool is used to secure the two ends of the press stud to the leather to allow opening and closing. See instructions on page 22.

Edge beveler

Use this tool to soften the edges of vegetable leather by removing the sharp edges of belts, straps, and handbag slings.

Skiving tool (also called a safety beveler)

This is used to skive off a layer of the leather on the flesh side to reduce the thickness or bulk. This comes in handy when leather is folded over or several layers are placed on top of one another.

Hand protector

When stitching leather, force is sometimes needed to push the needle through several layers. Use a hand protector to assist with this by pushing the back of the needle against the round metal part of the protector.

LEATHER

There are many different types of leather, but for the projects in this book we mainly used:

- Vegetable-tanned leather
- Upholstery leather (chrome-tanned)
- Side leather (chrome-tanned)
- Suede

It is very important to know that the front of the leather is called the grain side and the back is called the flesh side as you will be required to place the leather either grain or flesh side facing up when stitching the items.

Leather can be tanned (or colored) in many different ways. The most common methods are vegetable tanning and chrome tanning.

VEGETABLE-TANNED LEATHER

This is when a raw hide is turned into leather by using vegetable tannins pressed from various barks and nuts to tan the leather. This process makes leather that has greater body and firmness than chrome leather and is perfect for embossing, molding and hand-dyeing. This leather is great for belts, satchels, holsters, knife sheaths, saddles, and many other craft projects.

CHROME-TANNED LEATHER

Chrome leather is tanned with chromium salts, resulting in a product that feels supple and much softer than vegetable-tanned leather. This tanning process is also much quicker as the raw hide absorbs the salt very quickly. Chrome leathers are usually pre-dyed to create beautiful, even colors. Chrome leathers are finished in different ways for different uses, for example, upholstery, clothing, shoes, bags and purses, etc.

SUEDE

This is not really a separate type of leather, but a specific finish. The hide is finished by buffing, brushing, or grinding the surface of the flesh (inner) side to create a nap.

QUANTITY AND CUT

To decide how much leather you need for your project, take your prepared templates (see page 124) to the supplier to make sure that everything for a project fits on the hide.

When you lay out your templates on the leather, bear in mind that leather stretches from side to side (belly leather) but not from head to tail. Cut panels from head to tail for the least stretch and the most strength.

Leather hides are also cut in various ways. The drawings below illustrate the different cuts.

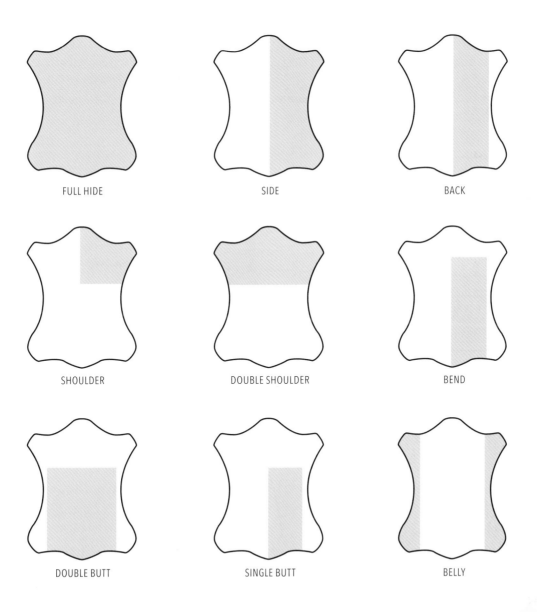

FULL HIDE

SIDE

BACK

SHOULDER

DOUBLE SHOULDER

BEND

DOUBLE BUTT

SINGLE BUTT

BELLY

Supplies

When working with leather you need a range of basic supplies to facilitate and finish the projects:

- **Spirit- or solvent-based dye** is used to dye vegetable-tanned leather. It is available in a variety of colors and should be used according to the manufacturer's instructions.
- **Water-based edge dye** is used to seal the edges of leather, creating a smooth edge.
- **Leather sealer** is applied over dyed leather to fix the color and protect the leather.
- **Waxed, braided thread** is used for hand-stitching as it doesn't fray and the thread is preserved. This is available in a wide variety of colors. You can use thread in a matching hue for the stitching, or try a contrasting color to add further embellishment. Always use enough thread to finish an entire seam or section.
- **Double-sided tape** is used to attach zippers to leather before they are stitched.

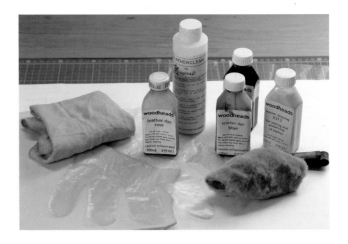

Adhesives

The projects in the book require a contact adhesive that is sprayed or brushed on. It is applied to both surfaces to be glued together, and left to become tacky (dry to the touch) before the two surfaces are brought together by applying pressure.

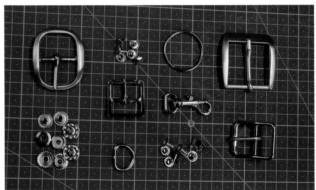

Hardware

- Rivets are used to permanently secure two pieces of leather together or as decorative elements.
- Buckles are used to open and adjust straps and belts. They come in a range of finishes and sizes, and each project mentions the specific buckle needed.
- Snap hooks or bolt snaps are used to clip straps to items.
- Press studs are used to allow opening and closing.
- Holster studs have the same functionality as a press stud but allow for adjustable sizing.
- Split rings are used as key rings.
- O-rings and D-rings are used to attach straps and slings to items.

TECHNIQUES

A few basic techniques are used for all the projects in this book, and once you have mastered these skills, you can really make anything you set your heart to.

PREPARING THE TEMPLATE

A scaled pattern is provided for each project and you are advised to use these to prepare a sturdy template for the item you are making.

1 Print all the pieces of the relevant pattern, enlarged to the specified scale (1:3 means 300% larger than the original), on standard 80 gsm paper. Most copy shops offer this service if your pattern pieces are larger than A4 or you do not have a printer.

2 Cut out each individual piece of the pattern leaving about 1 cm all round. Glue each part of the pattern to firm card stock and glue. I prefer using contact spray adhesive (use according to the manufacturer's instructions), but you can use any glue.

3 Using a metal ruler and an NT cutter, accurately cut out each piece of the pattern. Sometimes freehand cutting is required for curved shapes. A steady hand will go a long way here. You have now created the template that you will use to mark and cut out the leather.

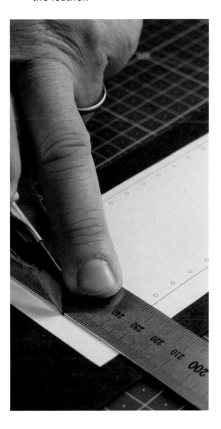

4 To complete the process, punch through each stitching hole marked on the template using junior punch pliers or a revolving punch (see page 10).

These holes will be used as stitch marks when assembling your leather item. If there are buckle slots, rivet holes, or stud holes and slits on your template, use a hollow slot punch (see page 11) to punch these into your paper template.

5 It is a good idea to keep all the pieces of a pattern together to prevent confusion when you start working on more than one project at a time. Either make a hole through all the pieces and tie a string through them or use a ziplock bag to keep them together.

MARKING THE LEATHER

1 Place your chosen piece of leather grain side up on a flat surface, preferably on a cutting board to protect your work surface.

2 Before you start marking and cutting, roughly place all the templates for one item to ensure that everything fits and that you are not wasting any leather.

3 Position the template flat on the leather, pushing down on it with one hand to prevent it from moving or shifting. Using a marking pen or scratch awl, trace the template onto the leather.

4 Still holding the template down firmly, mark all the stitching holes using a scratch awl. Push down firmly on the awl to ensure that the markings are clearly visible on the leather.

5 Other markings on the patterns are rivet holes, buckle slots, and stud holes and slits. Each of these is also marked on the leather using the marking pen.

If you are using pre-colored leather, skip the next process and go straight to punching the stitching holes and other markings and cutting the leather.

HAND-DYEING THE LEATHER

If you are using natural vegetable-tanned leather, you have the option of dyeing the leather the color that you want your final item to be. Here you have one of two choices: Either use a piece of leather big enough to accommodate all your templates, and dye that piece of leather all at once. Or, if you are using smaller, individual pieces of leather, you have the option of cutting out the leather from the templates first before dyeing each individual piece.

Note that you dye the leather before punching the stitching holes and other markings.

THE DYEING PROCESS

Vegetable-tanned leather is the most suitable type of leather for hand-dyeing. Both the grain and the flesh side of the leather can be dyed, depending on the look you want to create. The grain side gives a more even finish.

Different types of dyes give different finishes. For the purpose of this book we are using a spirit- or solvent-based dye for the surface and a water-based dye for the edges. The water-based dye will give you a smoother finish along the edges.

1 Thoroughly clean the leather using leather cleaner according to the manufacturer's instructions. Use a clean cloth and work on a dust-free surface.

2 Make sure that you have everything that you need handy before starting the dyeing process so that you don't have to stop in the middle.

3 Place a generous amount of dye on the applicator (use the dye as is, don't dilute it), start in the top corner and use circular movements to apply the dye to the leather. Each circle should slightly overlap the previous one for a smooth finish. If you see that the applicator is running dry, place more dye on it so that you can apply it evenly over the entire surface.

4 Once you have dyed the whole piece of leather, leave it to dry (this does not take very long). Once dry, you may note that some areas are darker than others. This is due to the application or the texture of the leather. Buff the leather thoroughly with a soft cloth to remove excess dye not absorbed by the leather. You can repeat the dyeing process a second or third time until the desired look is achieved.

5 Leave to dry again and then seal with a leather sealer.

6 Once you cut out the pattern pieces, you will have raw edges showing the white of the leather. Use a clothespin and felt brush to dye these edges. If you use spirit- or solvent-based dye for the edges, they need to be sealed after dyeing. It is not necessary to seal the edges if you use water-based dye.

TIP: There are other dyeing techniques, such as spray-dyeing and painting with a brush, but beginners are advised to stick to the hand-dyeing technique discussed here.

CUTTING THE LEATHER

The next step is to cut out all the pieces, working as accurately as you can. You need a cutting mat, a metal ruler, an NT cutter, and, optional for thinner leather, a pair of leather-cutting scissors. The most important requirement is that your cutting tools are sharp.

- Using a metal ruler and NT cutter and holding the knife firmly in your hand, stabilizing it with your forefinger on top of the knife, cut the leather along the tracing lines. Cut just inside the line to prevent any markings from showing on your leather pieces, but be careful not to reduce the size of the template.

- If the leather is thin enough, you can use leather-cutting scissors (note that these are not the same as normal fabric scissors—one of the blades is serrated).
- Do this with all the templates. Take note of the number of pieces that you need to cut of each template.
- When cutting curves, first cut a wider area, then edge closer to the actual curve. Don't rush.

- When you have to cut out a corner, always cut away from the corner until you are almost at the opposite side. Turn the leather around and cut away from the corner again to meet up with the cutting line.

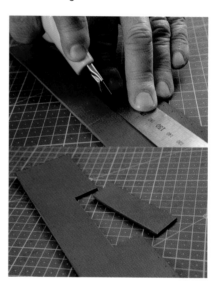

PUNCHING THE MARKINGS

There is a wide range of tools for cutting and punching the markings in the leather.

Stitching holes: These are the small holes that appear on every template and will be used to hand-stitch the different parts of your leather item together.

- Use the revolving punch pliers or junior punch pliers to punch the holes into the leather.

Rivet and stud holes: These holes are slightly bigger than stitching holes, and you can use the mini or maxi round-hole punch set (see page 11) or revolving punch pliers (see page 10) to punch these holes into the leather. The round-hole punch set is used when the marking cannot be reached with the revolving punch pliers.

- A round-hole punch is used by placing the leather on a nylon pad on a firm surface. Place the punch directly over the marked hole and use a nylon mallet to knock the punch through the leather. The reason for using a nylon pad and mallet is to prevent damage to your tools.

Buckle slots: These openings are for the prong of the buckle to slide through.

- Use a hollow slot punch (see page 11) to make these holes in the leather. Place the leather piece on a nylon pad on a firm surface. Place the punch directly over the marked hole and use a nylon mallet to knock the punch through the leather.

Belt tips and ends: These are created with punches to ensure a professional finish.

- To neatly shape the ends and tips of belts, use a belt tip or end punches. Place the belt on a nylon pad on a firm surface, place the punch in position on the leather and knock the punch through the leather with a nylon mallet.

ATTACHING A RIVET

Rivets can be set by using either a hammer and anvil or a rivet setter. The hammer will create a flat surface while the rivet setter will retain the dome shape of the cap.

• To fit the rivet, push the stem of the rivet through the rivet hole from the bottom. Place the cap over the stem and secure with the hammer or rivet setter.

SECURING PRESS STUDS

A press stud is used to fasten two sections of leather to allow for opening and closing. Make sure that you know which part of the press stud should be on which side of the leather (grain or flesh). A press stud consists of four parts: the post and stud (bottom parts) and the socket and button (top parts). Start with the leather section that will be at the bottom once the press stud is fastened.

1 Place the post into the anvil of the press-stud tool and position the leather (where the hole is) over the post.

2 Insert the stud into the cavity of the tool and place it over the protruding post.

3 Using a nylon mallet, hit down on the tool to connect the stud to the post.

4 To attach the other side of the press stud that will be at the top once fastened, place the button upside down into the anvil.

5 Place the hole in the leather over the stem of the button so that the stem protrudes through the press-stud hole.

6 Place the socket over the stem, insert the press-stud tool with the protruding prong into the hole of the socket and hit down on the tool with your nylon mallet to securely fix the press stud.

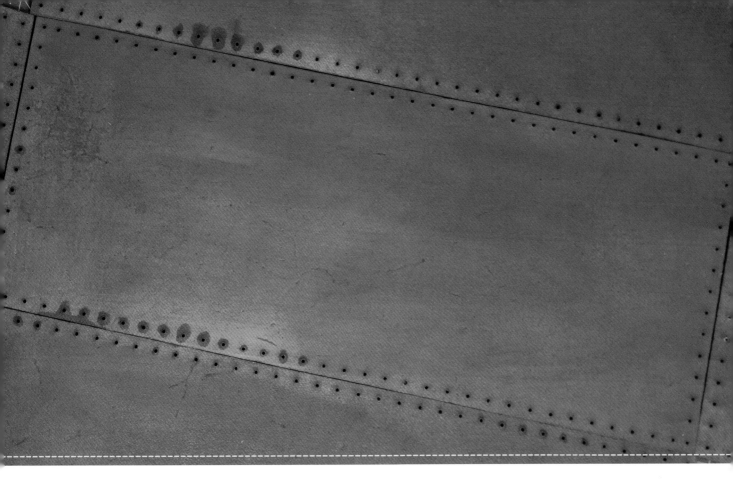

Stitches used to assemble leather items

A variety of stitches can be used depending on the purpose of the stitching and the look that you want to create. You will use harness or sail needles and waxed braided thread for the stitching (see page 12). Harness needles are used with most projects; if sail (sharp) needles are required, it will be specifically mentioned.

If the project requires the stitching to permanently hold the leather pieces together, saddle stitch, cross-stitch, and whipstitch are used. Whichever stitch you use, it is best to use enough thread to complete an entire seam or side without having to rethread and restart. This is for both durability and aesthetics.

Running stitch

This is used for decorative purposes only or if the sections do not need to be held in place by the stitching. This is just a basic straight stitch that is made by inserting the needle through the first hole, coming out at the second hole, in through the third hole, out through the fourth hole, and so on.

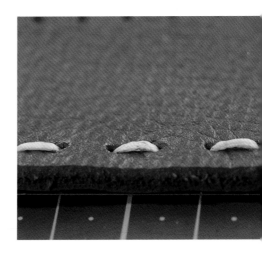

Saddle stitch

Saddle stitch is used to join two pieces of leather placed on top of each other. The stitch can be on the outside, where it will be both decorative and functional, or on the inside where it will be purely functional.

One way of making a saddle stitch is to use only one needle, sew a row of running stitches and then work back the same way, making stitches in the open areas between the stitches of the first row to complete the saddle stitch. This works well for short seams, but with longer seams you end up having to work with a very long piece of thread.

The method used in this book is sewing with two needles. To calculate the length of thread needed, use four times the length of the area that needs to be stitched. Cut the thread at an angle to make it easier to go through the needle.

1   Begin by threading a needle on both ends of the thread. Push one needle through the first stitching hole and pull the thread through halfway only. Make the first row of running stitches using one needle.

2   Once you get to the end, go back to where you started and make the second row of running stitches with the second needle (to form the saddle stitch).

3   To secure the end, once you get to the last hole, make a double stitch by stitching through the same two holes twice. Knot the two end pieces of the thread (double knot), cut off the ends, and burn them with a lighter or match to prevent the thread from fraying.

Saddle stitch and whipstitch

Saddle stitch and whipstitch are also used to join two pieces of leather that are placed on top of each other. The whipstitch adds both strength and a decorative element. When working the whipstitch, do not pull the thread too tight as this will cause the leather to pucker—especially softer leather.

1 Follow the same steps as for the saddle stitch and end off. Once you have completed the saddle stitch you will use one needle only and work a whipstitch back the way you came. Bring your needle over the edge and insert it from the top of the second hole to create a whipstitch. Repeat until you get to

the end of the area. Once you've inserted the needle through the last hole, form a double stitch and finish off by tying a knot and pulling it through into the leather.

2 Finish off the end where you started the whipstitch in the same way.

Cross-stitch

Cross-stitch is used mostly to secure two pieces of leather that need to be flush against each other (next to each other) or at an angle. You can also use one or two needles. Using one needle only, you sew until you get to the end of the seam, then work back to complete the crosses. The method used in this book is to sew with two needles simultaneously. To calculate the length of thread needed, use four to six times the length of the area that needs to be stitched.

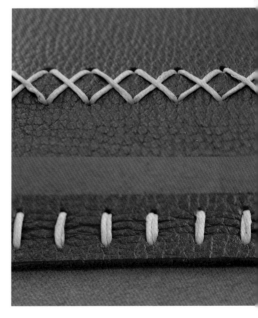

1 Begin by threading a needle on both ends of the thread. Push one needle through the first stitching hole in one piece of leather (from the back) and pull the thread through halfway only. Push the other needle through the first hole of the other piece of leather, also from the back.

2 Using the same needle that you started with, make a double loop through the same two starting holes to secure the beginning of the stitch.

3   Move the first needle down diagonally to the opposite, next hole on the other side and insert it from the front to the back.

4   At the back, move to the hole directly opposite the one you just came out of and insert the needle through from the back to the front.

5   Repeat steps 3 and 4 until you get to the end of the area that needs to be stitched.

6   Go back to the start and repeat steps 3 and 4 with the other needle working in the opposite direction to form the crosses.

7   Once you get to the last hole, make a double horizontal stitch (you do this with both needles). Tie a knot at the back of the leather to secure the stitching, cut off the remaining thread and burn the ends to prevent the thread from fraying.

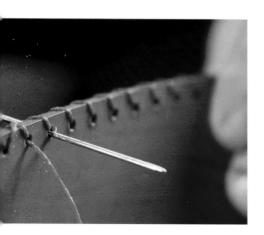

Decorative cross-stitch

This is often used around the top edge of a leather item. When decorative cross-stitch is sewn around the edge of an item, there is no need to start or end with a double loop through the same two top holes at each top corner.

Cross-stitch joining two panels at a 90-degree angle

One panel is usually lined up behind the other so that there aren't any rough edges. Follow the instructions for the individual projects closely.

CROSS-STITCH ATTACHING ONE PANEL AT A 90-DEGREE ANGLE

One panel is centered between two rows of stitching holes on another panel, forming a right angle, and incorporated when the back of the cross-stitch is made. Follow the instructions for the individual projects closely.

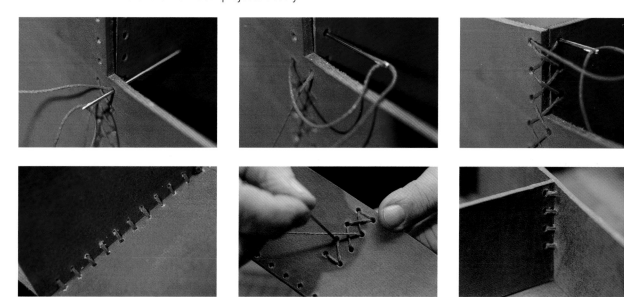

CROSS-STITCH INCLUDING A THIRD LAYER (BASE)

Cross-stitch to the bottom of the corner you are working on, then incorporate the third layer and continue stitching on the third layer.

ENDING OFF

In addition to ending off with a double stitch, bring the thread through to the back, or between layers, double knot and burn the edges to prevent fraying.

PROJECT PREPARATION

Preparation is key for successful and professional looking hand-stitched leather items. Follow these useful tips:

- When making sets, use leather from the same hide, if possible.
- Try to avoid marks or cuts in the leather when you lay out the templates.
- Dye all the leather for one project before you start tracing and cutting out templates.
- Make sure that you have the right color dye for the raw edges and use a clothespin and felt brush (see page 20) to facilitate the dyeing of the edges.
- When using different types of leather for the same project, make sure that the colors are a close match if not exactly the same. Alternatively you can use contrasting colors.
- Always use sharp tools when cutting and punching and use the appropriate backing to protect your tools.
- Check that all the stitching holes and other markings have been punched all the way through so that you don't have to open half-punched holes or remove bits of remaining leather while you are stitching.
- Where project instructions indicate that you have to make a fold in the edge of a panel before stitching, it helps to dampen the leather before making the fold.

PROJECTS

IN-BOX

XXXXXXXXXXXXXXXXXXXXXXXXXXXXXXXXXXXXXXXXXX

You will need

Vegetable leather dyed in the
    color of your choice
Templates on page 128
Cutting mat and cutting tools
Water-based dye
Felt and clothespin brush
2 harness needles
Thread

1 Prepare the templates according to the instructions on page 17.

2 Using the prepared templates, mark and cut out the leather, then stain the raw edges as explained on page 20.

3 Once you have punched all the stitching holes, place the base of the tray grain side up on your work surface.

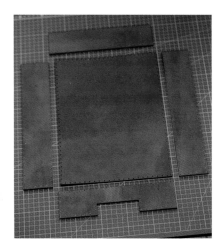

Place the two side panels as well as the front and back panels flesh side up next to the base with the stitching holes positioned next to each other. Don't be alarmed that the front and back panels are slightly longer than the base; this prevents a raw edge from showing in the corner.

4 Using enough thread for two short sides and one long side, thread up two needles. Line up the right-hand side panel behind the front panel at a 90-degree angle. Starting at the top of the corner, cross-stitch (see page 25) down to the bottom of the corner.

5 When you get to the bottom, add the base to your layers (see page 27) and cross-stitch across the front panel of the tray.

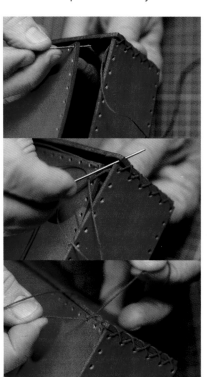

6 At the next corner, add the other side panel and sew up to the top. End off.

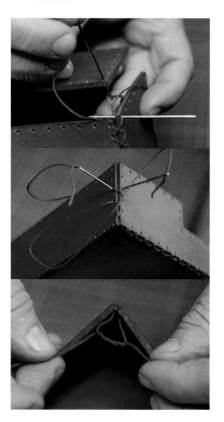

30

7 Go back to the bottom of the tray and, using a new piece of thread, sew the base of the tray to the side panel. At the next corner, add the back panel and sew up to the top. End off.

8 Go to the bottom of the back panel and sew it to the base of the tray. At the corner, sew up to the top and end off.

9 Repeat with the remaining side panel until you get back to the bottom of the first corner and end off.

10 Decorate the top edge of the tray with cross stitch.

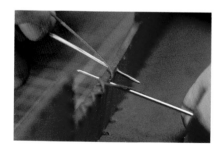

BUSINESS-CARD HOLDER

XXXXXXXXXXXXXXXXXXXXXXXXXXXXXXXXXXXXXXXXXXXXXXXXXXXX

You will need

Vegetable leather dyed in
  the color of your choice
Templates on page 160
Cutting mat and cutting tools
Water-based dye
Felt and clothespin brush
2 harness needles
Thread

1 Prepare the templates according to the instructions on page 17.

2 Using the prepared templates, mark and cut out the leather, then stain the raw edges as explained on page 20.

3 Once you have punched all the stitching holes, place the base of the business card holder flesh side up on your work surface. Place the two side panels as well as the front and back panels flesh side up next to the base with the stitching holes positioned next to each other. Don't be alarmed that the front and back panels are slightly longer than the base; this prevents a raw edge from showing in the corner.

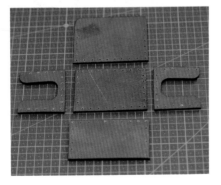

4 Line up the right-hand side panel behind the front panel at a 90-degree angle. Starting with a double stitch at the top, cross-stitch (see page 25) down to the bottom of the corner. When you get to the bottom, add the base to your layers and cross-stitch across the front panel of the card holder.

5 At the next corner, add the other side panel and sew up into the top. End off.

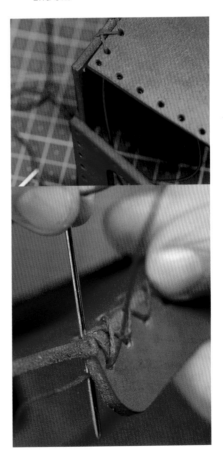

32

6 Go back to the bottom of the card holder and, using a new piece of thread, sew the base of the card holder to the side panel. At the next corner, add the back panel, sew up to the top of the corner and end off.

7 Go to the bottom of the back panel and sew it to the base of the card holder. At the next corner, sew up to the top and end off.

8 Repeat with the remaining side panel until you get back to the bottom of the first corner and end off.

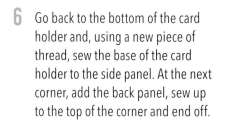

A4 DOCUMENT HOLDER

You will need

Vegetable leather dyed in
   the color of your choice
Side leather in the same color
Templates on page 129
Cutting mat and cutting tools
Water-based dye
Felt and clothespin brush
2 harness needles
Thread
3 9 mm (⅜ in.) rivets
Rivet setter
Hammer and anvil

1 Prepare the templates according to the instructions on page 17.

2 Using the prepared templates, mark and cut out the leather, taking note of the type of leather required for each piece, then stain the raw edges of the vegetable leather sections as explained on page 20.

3 Once you have punched all the stitching holes, place the pocket flesh side up on your work surface. Place the gusset grain side up at the top of the pocket, lining up the stitching holes. Start with a double stitch and saddle stitch (see page 24) the two pieces together. End off and repeat with the other gusset.

4 Place the pocket sleeve grain side up on your work surface. Place the pocket (with the gussets attached) flesh side up on the pocket sleeve, lining up the stitching holes with the inner row of the pocket sleeve stitching holes.

Saddle stitch the two pieces together and set aside.

5 Place the front of the document holder grain side up on your work surface. Attach the tab loop to the front by lining up the rivet holes and securing it with rivets (see page 22).

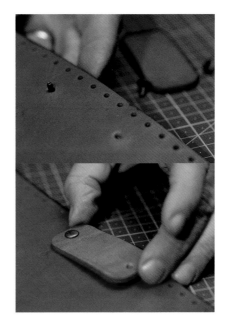

SEE PHOTOGRAPH OF OPEN FOLDER ON PAGE 33.

6 Place the back of the document holder grain side up on your work surface. Attach the tab strap to the back by lining up the rivet holes and securing it with a rivet.

7 Take the pocket and pocket sleeve that you've set aside, fold over the pocket and place it on the flesh side of the front panel, lining up the outside stitching holes (where the rivets are).

Starting in one of the outside corners, make one stitch and then fold the gusset toward you, positioning the first stitching hole of the gusset over the third hole of the pocket sleeve.

When you make your second stitch, you will include the gusset into your sewing. Keep on sewing until you reach the second to the last hole.

8   Saddle stitch the spine and the front panel together with the spine flesh side up. When you get to the other end of the spine, continue stitching over the front panel, and once you reach the sixth hole, add the pocket sleeve so that you include it in your layers from the seventh hole. When you reach the

fourth hole on the pocket sleeve, include the gusset in your layers. Continue sewing until you get back to where you started. Set this section aside.

9   Place the back of the document holder flesh side up on your work surface. Place the pad insert grain side up on the back panel. Starting in the bottom left-hand corner, leave one stitching hole open and sew along the short side of the folder, continue up the long side and complete the other short side, leaving open the last stitching hole. Don't end off. Place the spine on top of the back panel where the stitching holes are and continue stitching to join the front and back panels.

10   When sewing the spine to the back panel, position the pen holder where you want it. Fold it over to line up all the stitching holes (forming a loop for the pen) and sew through all the layers.

Continue until you get back to where you started and end off the stitching.

11   Close the document holder by sliding the tab through the tab loop.

SMALL BIN

✕✕✕

You will need

Vegetable leather dyed in the
   color of your choice
Templates on page 128
Cutting mat and cutting tools
Water-based dye
Felt and clothespin brush
2 harness needles
Thread

1 Prepare the templates according to
the instructions on page 17.

2 Using the prepared templates,
mark and cut out the leather, then
stain the raw edges as explained
on page 20.

3 Once you have punched all the
stitching holes, place the base of
the bin flesh side up on your work
surface with the four side panels
flesh side up next to the base with
the stitching holes positioned next
to each other.

Don't be alarmed that two of the
panels are slightly longer than the
base. This is the front and the back
of your bin (make sure they are
placed in the correct positions).

4 Place the left-hand side panel behind the front (slightly longer) panel to form the corner. With two needles threaded with enough thread for two sides and one base, start at the top of the corner and cross-stitch (see page 25) down to the bottom. Add the base to your layers and join the front to the base.

5 At the next corner, add the right-hand side panel, and sew up to the top of the corner and end off.

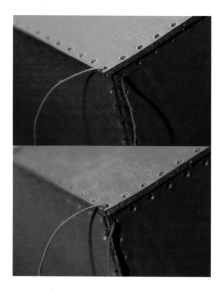

6 Using a new piece of thread, go back to the bottom of the bin and sew the base to the right-hand side panel. At the next corner, add the back panel, sew to the top of the corner and end off.

7 Go to the bottom of the back panel and sew it to the base until you get to the next corner. Sew up into the corner and end off.

8 Sew the base to the bottom of the left-hand side panel and end off.

9 To finish the bin, use cross stitch to decorate the top of the bin (see page 26).

38

DESK BLOTTER

✕✕

1 Prepare the templates according to the instructions on page 17.

2 Using the prepared templates, mark and cut out the leather, taking note of the type of leather required for each piece, then stain the raw edges of the vegetable leather sections as explained on page 20.

3 Once you have punched all the stitching holes, place the side piece on top of the side lining (grain sides together), lining up the rectangle of stitching holes.

4 Saddle stitch (see page 24) the two pieces together and repeat with the other side piece and lining.

5 Place the base of the blotter grain side up on your work surface. Position the side lining (with side piece attached) under the short side of the base (flesh side facing) and line up the single line of stitching holes with the stitching holes of the base.

6 Start at the top and saddle stitch the two sections together.

7 When you get to the bottom, continue the saddle stitching along the long side of the base. When you get to the side, position the other side lining under the base and continue sewing to the top, then along the other long side until you get back to where you started.

STATIONERY TRAY

You will need

Vegetable leather dyed in the color of your choice
Templates on page 137
Cutting mat and cutting tools
Water-based dye
Felt and clothespin brush
2 harness needles
Thread

1 Prepare the templates according to the instructions on page 17.

2 Using the prepared templates, mark and cut out the leather, then stain the raw edges as explained on page 20.

3 Once you have punched all the stitching holes, place the short divider with the grain side facing to the right in the center of the two rows of stitching holes behind the long divider with the grain side facing the front and make them stand upright.

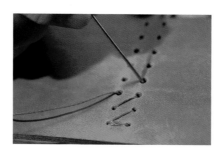

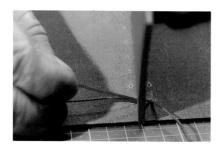

4 Start with a double stitch at the bottom where the two dividers meet at a 90-degree angle and cross-stitch the two panels together using

a flat cross-stitch (see page 25). When one section falls away with three holes left, continue sewing the two panels together until you get to the top. End off and set aside.

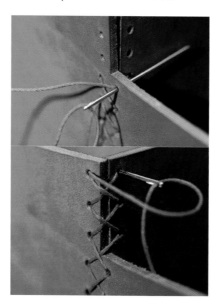

5 Place the base of the tray flesh side up on your work surface. Place the front and back panels as well as the two side panels flesh side up next to the base with the stitching holes positioned next to one another.

One side panel is higher than the other one. Place the higher one on the left of the base.

6 Place the right-hand side panel behind the front panel to form the corner.

7 Starting at the top of the corner, cross-stitch down until you get to the bottom. When you reach the bottom, add the base to your layers and cross-stitch across the front of the tray.

8   At the next corner, add the other side panel, sew up to the top of the corner and end off.

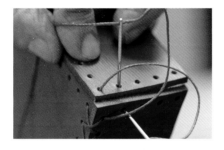

9   Go back to the bottom of the tray and, using a new piece of thread, sew the base of the tray to the side panel. At the next corner, add the back panel, sew up to the top of the corner and end off.

10   Go to the bottom of the back panel and sew it to the base of the tray. At the next corner, sew up to the top and end off. Then sew the remaining side panel to the base and end off.

11   Place the two dividers in the middle of the tray with the long one in front and centered between the stitching holes in the side

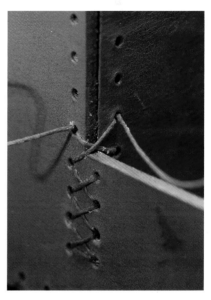

panels, the short one centered between the stitching holes in the back panel. Following the same technique as when you joined the two dividers, attach the dividers to the back and the sides of the tray, always starting at the bottom.

PENCIL BAG

XXXXXXXXXXXXXXXXXXXXXXXXXXXXXXXXXXXXXXXXX

You will need

Side leather
Templates on page 131
Cutting mat and cutting tools
20 cm (7⅞ in.) zipper
5 mm (⅕ in.) double-sided
     tape
2 harness needles
2 sail needles
Thread

1   Prepare the templates according to the instructions on page 17.

2   Using the prepared templates, mark and cut out the leather, then punch all the stitching holes and cut out the zipper opening.

3   Place the base of the pencil bag flesh side up on your work surface. Arrange the triangular panels as well as the two rectangular panels (also flesh side up) in position around the base with the stitching holes positioned next to each other.

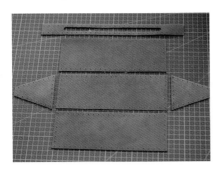

4   Place a triangle and a rectangle flesh sides together, lining up the short sides. Starting at the top, sew cross-stitches (see page 25) down

to the bottom, add the base to your layers and cross-stitch along the long side of the base.

5   At the next corner, add the other triangle, sew up to the top of the corner and end off.

6   Go back to the bottom of the bag and, using a new piece of thread, sew the base of the bag to the triangular panel. At the next corner, add the rectangle, sew up to the top of the corner and end off.

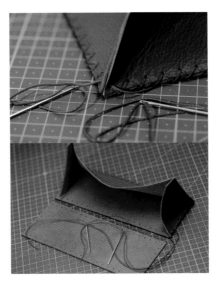

7   Go to the bottom of the rectangle and sew it to the base of the bag. At the next corner, join the triangle, sew up to the top and end off.

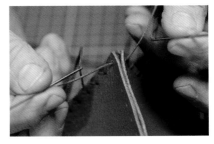

8   Sew the remaining short side of the base to the triangle and end off.

9   On the face of the zipper adhere double-sided tape to both edges. Position the top of the bag grain side up with the zipper opening over the zipper and glue down,

leaving four stitching holes on
either side of the top panel free.

10 Fold over the leather end pieces
so that the first two stitching holes
line up over the next two stitching
holes, closing the zipper ends.

11 Start with a double side stitch and
make one cross-stitch. When you
make the second stitch, include the
body of the bag and sew one side
of the top panel to the bag.

12 When you get to the other end, fold
over the end piece lining up the
last four stitching holes. End with
a double side stitch, then push the
needle through one layer of the
folded-over piece so that it exits
from the inside. Make a knot, cut
off the long pieces of the thread,
and push the knot and threads
into the fold using a scratch awl
or the needle.

13 Repeat on the other side.

FIREWOOD CARRIER

You will need

- Vegetable leather dyed in the color of your choice
- Side leather in the same color
- Templates on page 132
- Cutting mat and cutting tools
- Water-based dye
- Felt and clothespin brush
- 2 harness needles
- Thread
- 18 9 mm (3/8 in.) rivets
- Hammer and anvil

1 Prepare the templates according to the instructions on page 17.

2 Using the prepared templates, mark and cut out the leather, then stain the raw edges as explained on page 20, and punch all the stitching and rivet holes.

3 Place the base of the carrier grain side up on your work surface. Place one of the side panels grain side up over the base, lining up the stitching holes.

4 Rivet (see page 22) the two pieces of leather together using four rivets. This will facilitate the stitching as the pieces are already securely in place.

5 Saddle stitch (see page 24) the two pieces together (through both rows of stitching holes), starting with an overstitch.

6 Make a fold in the middle of one handle, grain sides together, and attach two rivets.

7 Saddle stitch across the opening from one rivet to the next. Start by inserting the needle between the two layers and making an overstitch. End off by inserting the needle between the two layers again, making a knot and pushing it back between the layers.

8 Place the end of the handle strap on the grain side of the side panel, ensuring that all the holes are lined up correctly. Set the four rivets and follow up with saddle stitch to secure the handle to the carrier. Repeat on the other side.

9 Repeat steps 6–8 for the other handle.

TWO-BOTTLE WINE CARRIER

You will need

Vegetable leather dyed in the
    color of your choice
Templates on page 133
Cutting mat and cutting tools
Water-based dye
Felt and clothespin brush
2 harness needles
Thread
30 mm (1⅕ in.) half buckle
4 9 mm (⅜ in.) rivets
1 7 mm (¼ in.) rivet
Rivet setter
Hammer and anvil

1 Prepare the templates according to the instructions on page 17.

2 Using the prepared templates, mark and cut out the leather, then stain the raw edges as explained on page 20, and punch all the stitching and rivet holes.

3 Place the base and two side panels grain side up on your work surface. Using just your hands, make a fold line about 1 cm (²/₅ in.) from the edge on the long sides of all three panels.

4 Place a side panel over one short side of the base and line up the stitching holes. Join the short sides of the two pieces by saddle stitching (see page 24) between the slits, skipping one hole on either side, then repeat with the other side panel.

5 Place the handle on the side panel, lining up the rivet holes, and attach with a rivet (see page 22).

Saddle stitch the handle to the side panel, starting above the rivet, starting and ending with double stitches. Taking care not to twist the handle, attach the other end to the other side panel in the same way and set aside.

6 Place the closing strap grain side up on the grain side of the back panel flap. Line up the rivet holes and attach the strap with a rivet, then saddle stitch it to the back panel.

7 On the divider, dampen the leather and make a fold line 1 cm (²/₅ in.) from the edge with the stitching holes. Placing the divider so that the bottom hole on the back panel is open, line up its stitching holes with the middle row of stitching holes on the back panel, flesh sides together, and saddle stitch.

10 Place the buckle tab on the grain side of the front panel, lining up the rivet holes, and secure with a rivet. Saddle stitch the buckle tab to the front panel.

12 Starting at the top of one side, saddle stitch the panels together and end off when you get to the top of the other side.

13 Attach the front panel to the assembled back and side panels by lining up the stitching holes (ensure that the buckle faces up) and saddle stitching the base and sides.

8 Make the buckle loop by joining the ends with a 7 mm (¼ in.) rivet.

9 Slide the short side of the buckle tab through the buckle until the prong fits through the buckle slot. Fold over the tab, then slide in the loop from the long end.

11 Position the joined base and side panels over the back panel with the divider attached, flesh sides together. Fold the panel at the bottom to create a box shape at the bottom of the wine carrier. The slits in the side panels now create the base corners of the wine carrier.

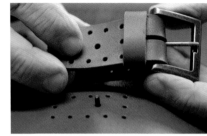

ADJUSTABLE BBQ APRON

XXXXXXXXXXXXXXXXXXXXXXXXXXXXXXXXXXXXXXXXXXXXXX

You will need

Side leather
Templates on page 134
Cutting mat and cutting tools
2 harness needles
Thread
2 25 mm (1 in.) roller buckles
2 7 mm (¼ in.) rivets
Hammer and anvil

1   Prepare the templates according to the instructions on page 17.

2   Using the prepared templates, mark and cut out the leather, then punch the buckle slots and the stitching and rivet holes.

3   Fold over the top of the front pocket (toward the flesh side), lining up the holes, and saddle stitch (see page 24).

4   Line up the pocket stitching holes with those on the body of the apron (grain sides up) and saddle stitch the pocket to the body, starting with a double overstitch. Repeat steps 3 and 4 for the pen pocket.

5   Slide a buckle tab through a buckle with the prong in the buckle slot. Fold the buckle tab over and secure it with a rivet (see page 22) just below the prong. Repeat with the other buckle tab.

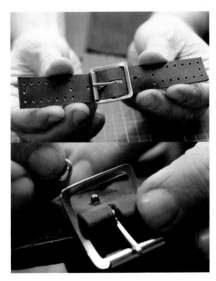

6   With the apron grain side up, place the right-hand side tab on the apron, also grain side up, aligning the stitching holes. Separate the two ends of a prepared buckle tab with one end going under the apron and the other over the side tab, aligning the stitching holes at the bottom of the side tab (the roller of the buckle needs to face away from the body of the apron).

7   Starting at the buckle end, saddle stitch the buckle tab and side tab to the apron.

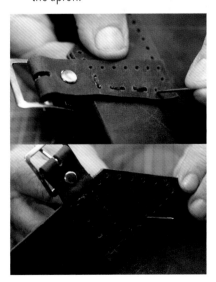

49

8 Place the left-hand side tab on the apron, aligning the stitching holes, followed by the body strap, aligning the stitching holes at the bottom of the side tab. Saddle stitch the strap and side tab to the apron.

9 With both pieces grain side up, place the neck lining in position at the neck edge of the apron and saddle stitch along the outer edge. The inside stitching holes are for the buckle tab and strap.

10 Attach the buckle tab with a saddle stitch, separating the two ends with one end going under the apron and the other over the neck lining and the roller of the buckle facing away from the apron.

11 Stitch the neck strap to the apron following the stitching holes.

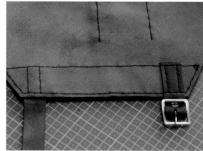

DICE CUP

XXXXXXXXXXXXXXXXXXXXXXXXXXXXXXXXXXXXXXXXXXXXXXXXX

You will need

Vegetable leather dyed in the color of your choice
Templates on page 132
Cutting mat and cutting tools
Water-based dye
Felt and clothespin brush
2 harness needles
Thread

1 Prepare the templates according to the instructions on page 17.

2 Using the prepared templates, mark and cut out the leather, then stain the raw edges as explained on page 20, and punch all the stitching holes.

3 Dampen the base of the dice cup to make it moldable. Place it grain side up and fold over the outside edge.

4 Push the side edges of the body of the cup flush against each other (grain side out). Starting at the top (where the opening is wider) cross-stitch the two ends together, but make sure that the crosses are on the inside and not on the outside as this ensures a tighter joint.

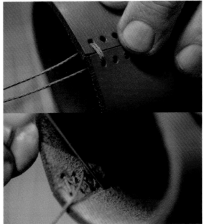

5 When you get to the last hole, insert the molded base into the opening with the grain side facing out and join the two pieces using a saddle stitch.

Jewelry box

You will need

Vegetable leather dyed in the
color of your choice
Templates on page 135
Cutting mat and cutting tools
Water-based dye
Felt and clothespin brush
2 harness needles
Thread

Box

1   Prepare the templates according to the instructions on page 17.

2   Using the prepared templates, mark and cut out the leather, then stain the raw edges as explained on page 20, and punch all the stitching holes.

3   Place one short divider at a 90-degree angle against the long divider, centered between two rows of stitching holes at the top. Start at the top and cross-stitch (see page 25) the two panels together. Repeat with the other short divider and set aside.

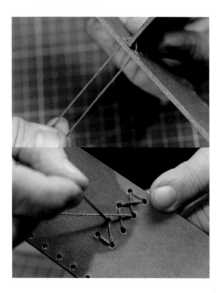

4   Join the box front, sides, base, and back following steps 4 to 9 of the in-box (see pages 30–31) but starting with the side aligned next to the front panel, not behind.

5   Place the joined dividers into the box with the short ones facing the front and centered between the stitching holes. Following the same technique as when you joined the dividers, sew the short panels to the front of the box, starting at the top.

6   Sew the long divider to the side panels using the same technique.

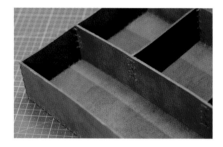

Lid

Repeat step 4 to make the box lid, but starting with the side panel lined up behind the front panel.

PHOTO BOX

BOX

1 Prepare the templates according to the instructions on page 17.

2 Using the prepared templates, mark and cut out the leather, then stain the raw edges as explained on page 20, and punch all the stitching holes.

3 Join the box front, sides, base, and back following steps 4 to 9 of the in-box (see pages 30–31).

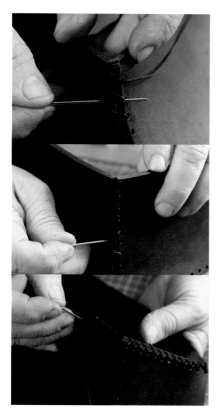

LID

1 Prepare the templates according to the instructions on page 17.

2 Using the prepared templates, mark and cut out the leather, then stain the raw edges as explained on page 20, and punch all the stitching and rivet holes.

3 Make the lid in exactly the same way as the box.

4 Cut the plastic window and fabric using the templates. Also cut the lid lining from card stock. When you remove the center, work carefully and accurately as you will be using the cutout.

5 Adhere 8 mm (1/3 in.) double-sided tape to all the sides of the plastic window.

6 Remove the tape backing and glue the plastic to the inside of

You will need

Vegetable leather dyed in the color of your choice
Templates on page 136
Cutting mat and cutting tools
Water-based dye
Felt and clothespin brush
2 harness needles
2 sail needles
Thread
A4 heavy-duty plastic or acetate film
A4 card stock (170–210 gsm)
2 7 mm (1/4 in.) rivets
8mm double-sided tape
Block print fabric scrap (178 231 mm / 7 9 1/16 in.)
Contact spray adhesive
Hammer and anvil

the lid so that it covers the window opening, fitting neatly inside the stitching holes.

7 Place the cutout in the lid lining, closing the window opening. Apply contact spray adhesive to the entire lid lining and cover it with the block print fabric, carefully smoothing it down with your fingers to avoid air bubbles and creases.

8　Turn the lining over and, using an NT cutter, cut through the fabric backing along two short sides and the long side where the rivet holes for the two slide locks of the window opening are. Leave the other long side intact as this will form the hinge.

9　Turn the lining over, print side facing up. Place the slide locks over the rivet holes and secure them in place with two rivets. Don't tighten the rivets too much as the slide lock must be able to turn.

10　Adhere double-sided tape to the back of the lining and paste it into the lid, print side facing up.

11　Saddle stitch the lining to the lid using the sail needles so that you can easily pierce the fabric as there are no stitching holes.

TWO-POCKET SATCHEL

You will need

Vegetable leather dyed in the
color of your choice
Templates on page 142
Cutting mat and cutting tools
Water-based dye
Felt and clothespin brush
2 harness needles
Thread
2 16 mm (⅝ in.) roller buckles
1 25 mm (1 in.) roller buckle
2 20 mm (⅞ in.) D-rings
2 25 mm (1 in.) D-rings
4 9 mm (⅜ in.) rivets
Hammer and anvil

1 Prepare the templates according to the instructions on page 17.

2 Using the prepared templates, mark and cut out the leather, then stain the raw edges as explained on page 20, and punch all the stitching holes, buckle holes, and slots and rivet holes.

PREPARING AND ATTACHING THE HANDLE

3 With the handle skin side up, slide a 20 mm (⅞ in.) D-ring over each end and position it where there is a gap in the stitching holes. Fold over one end of the handle, lining up the stitching holes. Repeat with the other end so that all the holes line up (this will form the handle grip).

4 Saddle stitch through all three layers, securing the ends with double side stitches.

5 Slide the narrow end of one handle tab through the D-ring on the grip. Fold over the end and place the handle tab on the grain side of the back and flap where the stitching holes are. Secure with a rivet and saddle stitch through all three layers and repeat on the other side.

ATTACHING THE FLAP STRAPS

6 Place the flap strap on the back and flap where the stitching holes are, long end extending over the side.

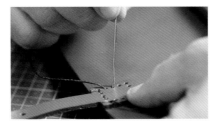

7 Saddle stitch one the flap strap to the back and flap, making a double overstitch on both sides of the strap. Repeat with the other strap.

ATTACHING THE FRONT POCKETS

8 Slide a buckle tab through the 16 mm (⅝ in.) buckle until the prong fits through the buckle slot. Fold the narrow end over, place the buckle tab on the grain side of the pocket where the stitching holes are and saddle stitch the three layers together. Leave the bottom row open.

9 Using your hands, make a folding line on both the long sides of the gusset (grain side up). Place the gusset on the pocket, flesh sides together. Saddle stitch, starting and ending with a side stitch.

10 Place the pocket and gusset on the grain side of the front panel, making sure that the gusset fold remains in place. Saddle stitch the pocket to the front panel, starting and ending with an overstitch, then repeat with the other pocket.

ATTACHING THE SLING TABS

11 Place the bag gusset grain side up on your work surface. Using your hands, make a folding line in both the long sides of the gusset.

12 Slide the narrow end of the sling tab through the 25 mm D-ring.

Fold the end over the rounding of the D-ring and place onto the gusset where the stitching holes are. Secure with a rivet and saddle stitch all three layers together, then repeat on the other side.

ASSEMBLING THE BAG

13 Place the gusset on the front panel, flesh sides together and saddle stitch, starting and ending with an overstitch.

14 Attach the back and flap panel in the same way with saddle stitching, starting and ending with a side stitch.

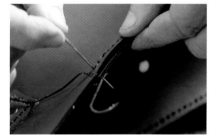

ATTACHING THE STRAP

15 Slide the end of the sling buckle strap through the 25 mm (1 in.) buckle until the prong fits through the buckle slot. Fold the buckle strap over and saddle stitch the two layers together, securing the four corners with a side stitch.

16 Slide the other end of the sling buckle strap through the D-ring on the gusset. Fold it over and sew the two layers together in the same way.

17 Secure the end of the sling strap to the D-ring on the other side of the gusset in the same way and fasten the buckle, adjusting the strap length.

LAPTOP BAG

XXXXXXXXXXXXXXXXXXXXXXXXXXXXXXXXXXXXXXXXXXXXXXXXXXXXXX

You will need

Vegetable leather dyed in the color of your choice
Upholstery leather in a matching color
Templates on page 143
Cutting mat and cutting tools
Water-based dye
Felt and clothespin brush
2 harness needles
2 sail needles
Thread
30 cm (11 ⅞ in.) zipper
25 mm (1 in.) half buckle
1 9 mm (⅜ in.) rivet
Contact adhesive and paintbrush
Double-sided tape
Hammer and anvil

1 Prepare the templates according to the instructions on page 17.

2 Using the prepared templates, mark and cut out the leather, including the zipper opening, then stain the raw edges as explained on page 20, and punch all the stitching holes and buckle holes and slots.

3 Adhere double-sided tape along both edges on the face side of the zipper. Remove the tape backing and place the front panel over the zipper (grain side up). Use the sail needles and saddle stitch the zipper to the panel, making double stitches on both short sides.

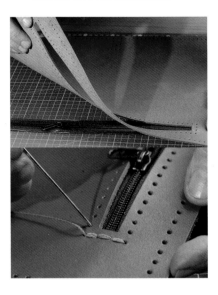

4 Close the loop with a rivet. Slide the buckle tab through the buckle until the prong fits through the buckle slot. Slide the loop in from the bottom until it reaches the buckle then fold over the back of the tab until the stitching holes line up.

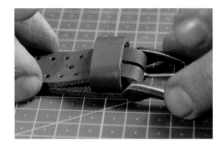

5 Place the buckle tab on the bag front, lining up the stitching and rivet holes, and rivet the three layers together.

6 Saddle stitch through all three layers to further secure the tab to the bag, using side stitches at the buckle end of the tab.

7 Turn both the front panel and the front zipper pocket lining flesh side up and apply contact adhesive along the edges, taking care not to cover the stitching holes.

8   Adhere the lining to the front panel with the stitching holes aligned. Lightly tap the edges with a hammer to set the glue, then saddle stitch the top of the panel above the zipper.

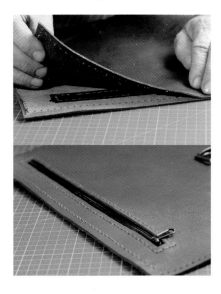

9   Place the gusset flesh side up on your work surface. Using just your hands, make a fold line about 1 cm (²⁄₅ in.) from the edge on the long sides of the gusset.

10 With the grain side of both panels up, line up the stitching holes of the gusset and the front panel. Starting at the top, saddle stitch down, across the bottom (over the buckle tab) and up the other side.

11 To attach the back, saddle stitch across the top of the gusset, align the back panel stitching holes with those on the other side of the gusset and continue stitching down, across the bottom and up the other side. Take the stitching across the other short side of the gusset as well.

12 Align the stitching holes of the buckle strap with those on the flap and attach the strap with saddle stitching.

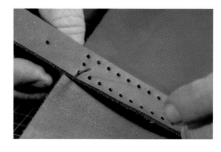

13 Attach the sling to the gusset on both sides using a saddle stitch. Double stitch the top row to strengthen the stitching.

BACKPACK

ⓧⓧⓧⓧⓧⓧⓧⓧⓧⓧⓧⓧⓧⓧⓧⓧⓧⓧⓧⓧⓧⓧⓧⓧⓧⓧⓧⓧⓧ

You will need

Vegetable leather dyed in the
   color of your choice
Templates on page 126
Cutting mat and cutting tools
Water-based dye
Felt and clothespin brush
2 harness needles
Thread
3 30 mm (1$\frac{1}{5}$ in.) half buckles
2 30 mm (1$\frac{1}{5}$ in.) D-rings
8 9 mm ($\frac{3}{8}$ in.) rivets
Hammer and anvil

1   Prepare the templates according to the instructions on page 17.

2   Using the prepared templates, mark and cut out the leather, then stain the raw edges as explained on page 20, and punch all the stitching holes, buckle slots, and rivet holes.

3   Place the bottom of the back panel over the bottom of the front panel (both grain side up), lining up the two rows of stitching holes. Cross-stitch the two panels together.

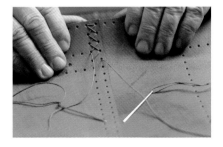

4   Close the three buckle loops with rivets and prepare the buckle tabs.

5   Slide the buckle tab (the end with the least number of stitching holes) through the buckle until the prong fits through the buckle slot. Slide the loop in from the bottom until it reaches the buckle.

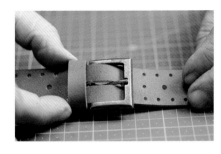

6   Fold over the shorter end, lining up the rivet holes, and place the buckle tab on the back panel where the stitching holes are, lining up the holes. Attach the tab with a rivet and saddle stitch right around through all the layers, making a double row of stitches closest to the buckle.

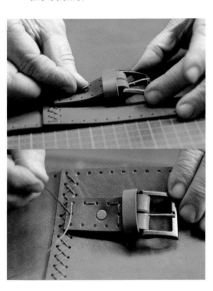

7   Repeat with the buckle tab on the other side, then attach the third buckle tab to the front pocket with the buckle facing the short side without stitching holes.

8   Place the pocket flesh side up on the body of the bag (grain side up) with the top of the pocket (with no holes) facing the handle. Line up the bottom row of stitching holes on the pocket with the short row of stitching holes on the front panel and saddle stitch.

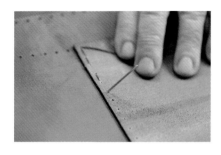

9 Attach the pocket gusset strap to the pocket gusset, grain sides together, lining up the edges and the stitching holes on one long side. Saddle stitch, starting with an overstitch.

Manipulate the leather around the curve at the bottom and stitch all the way to the other end. Dampen the gusset strap and shape it with a hammer, then repeat with the second gusset.

10 Place the assembled gusset with the gusset strap flesh side down on the pocket stitching holes on the front panel (grain side up).

Starting with an overstitch, saddle stitch the gusset to the front panel.

When you reach the bottom curve, fold over the pocket and continue stitching the gusset to the pocket, making sure that the stitching holes are aligned. Repeat on the other side.

11 Align the short rows of stitching holes at the top of the body gusset, grain sides together, and saddle stitch along the slit, then flatten the seam with a hammer.

12 Assemble the body gussets in the same way as the pocket gussets and attach to the assembled front and back panels using the same steps you followed to insert the pocket gussets. Start with the front and flip the back panel over when you reach the bottom curve, then stitch up to the end of the stitching holes in the back panel. Remember to start and end with an overstitch.

13 Aligning the flap strap with the rivet and stitching holes on the flap, attach it with a rivet, then secure with a saddle stitch, making two double stitches at the bottom.

14 Place the flap on the body, flesh sides together, aligning the handles and all the stitching and rivet holes.

15 Saddle stitch the flap to the body. First sew the long, straight row under the handle, making a side stitch on both sides.

Stitch around the flap curve and when you reach the handle, flip the handle flap through the opening and over so that the stitching holes line up, then continue the saddle stitch until you get back to where you started.

16 Slide the shoulder strap tab through the D-ring. Fold the tab over the straight bar and position it over the stitching holes next to the handle with the flap between the two ends.

Attach the tab to the flap with a rivet and secure with a saddle stitch, using double stitches closest to the bar. Repeat with the other shoulder strap tab.

17 Slide the shoulder strap through the D-ring, fold over the end and secure with a rivet and repeat on the other side.

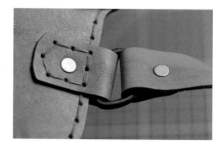

18 Fit the strap ends through the buckles.

SMALL SLING BAG

✕✕✕✕✕✕✕✕✕✕✕✕✕✕✕✕✕✕✕✕✕✕✕✕✕✕✕✕✕✕✕✕✕✕✕✕✕✕

You will need

Vegetable leather dyed in the
   color of your choice
Templates on page 144
Cutting mat and cutting tools
Water-based dye
Felt and clothespin brush
2 harness needles
Thread
2 15 mm ($^3/_5$ in.) D-rings
2 15 mm ($^3/_5$ in.) roller buckle
6 8 mm ($^1/_3$ in.) rivets
Hammer and anvil

1   Prepare the templates according to the instructions on page 17.

2   Using the prepared templates, mark and cut out the leather, then stain the raw edges as explained on page 20, and punch all the stitching holes, buckle slots, and rivet holes.

3   Prepare the sling by sliding the buckle strap into the buckle until the prong fits through the buckle slot. Fold over the end and secure with a rivet.

4   Slide the tab end of the gusset through the D-ring, fold over and secure with a rivet. Repeat on the other side.

5   Slide the narrow end of the buckle tab through the buckle until the prong fits through the buckle slot.

Fold over the end, place the buckle strap on the grain side of the front panel lining up the rivet holes and attach with a rivet through all three layers. Secure with a saddle stitch along the stitching holes.

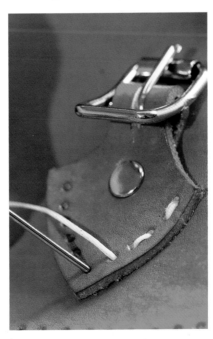

6   Place the closing strap grain side up on the grain side of the body and saddle stitch in place, starting and ending with an overstitch.

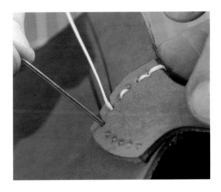

7   Make a folding line with your fingers in the long sides of the gusset (grain side up).

8 Lining up the stitching holes, position the gusset on the body, flesh sides together, and saddle stitch the gusset to the body.

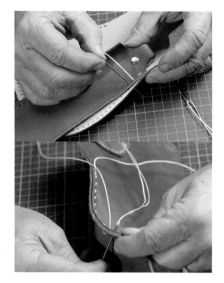

9 Place the front panel on the gusset, flesh sides together. Starting and ending with an overstitch, saddle stitch the gusset to the front.

10 Attach the buckle strap and sling strap to the D-rings by folding over the ends and securing with rivets.

WRIST STRAP

XXXXXXXXXXXXXXXXXXXXXXXXXXXXXXXXXXXXXXXXXXXXXXXXXXXXX

You will need

Vegetable leather dyed in the
   color of your choice
Templates on page 138
Cutting mat and cutting tools
Water-based dye
Felt and clothespin brush
1 press stud
Press-stud tool
Mallet

1 Prepare the template according to
   the instructions on page 17.

2 Using the prepared template,
   mark and cut out the leather, then
   stain the raw edges as explained
   on page 20, and punch the press-
   stud holes.

3 Attach the press studs on either
   side of the wrist strap following the
   instructions on page 22.

69

12-STRING ARMBAND

You will need

Vegetable leather dyed in the
    color of your choice
Template on page 127
Cutting mat and cutting tools
Water-based dye
Felt and clothespin brush
Steel ruler
NT cutter
2 press studs
Press-stud tool
Mallet

1 Prepare the template according to the instructions on page 17.

2 Using the prepared template, mark and cut out the leather, then stain the raw edges as explained on page 20, and punch the press-stud holes.

3 Use a steel ruler and an NT cutter to cut the strings along the lines that you marked when you prepared the leather.

4 Cut accurately, leaving 2.5 cm (1 in.) on each side of the strings intact. This is where the press studs will be attached.

5 Attach the press studs following the instructions on page 22.

WRAP-AROUND WRIST STRAP

You will need

Vegetable leather dyed in the
    color of your choice
Template on page 138
Cutting mat and cutting tools
Water-based dye
Felt and clothespin brush

1   Prepare a template for the slit end
    of the wrist strap according to the
    instructions on page 17.

2   Using the prepared template, mark
    and cut out the leather, extending
    the narrow end to your preferred
    measurement, then stain the raw
    edges as explained on page 20.

3   Punch the four holes where the
    markings are and cut between the
    holes as indicated on the pattern.
    This will form the slit where you will
    close the strap.

4   You can also use a softer leather
    to make this wrist strap using the
    same technique (leaving out the
    dye step).

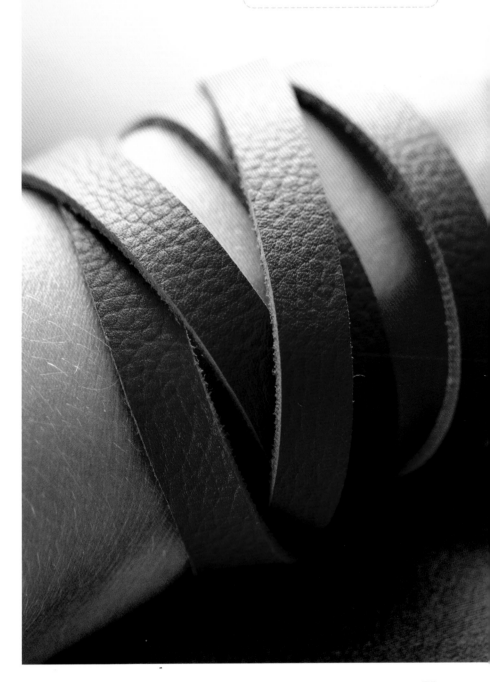

FRINGED NECKPIECE

You will need

Upholstery leather
Template on page 124
Cutting mat and cutting tools
Matching ribbon, thong,
   or cord
Cord ends
Fastener
Pliers

1   Prepare the template according to the instructions on page 17.

2   Using the prepared template, mark and cut out the leather and punch the ribbon/cord holes (see page 21).

3   Use a steel ruler and NT cutter to cut the fringes following the markings on the leather.

4   Measure the length of ribbon, cord, or thong that you will need to fasten the neckpiece around your neck. Push the ends through the holes from the back and make a knot on the front.

5   Halve the ribbon and attach the cord ends and fastener using the pliers.

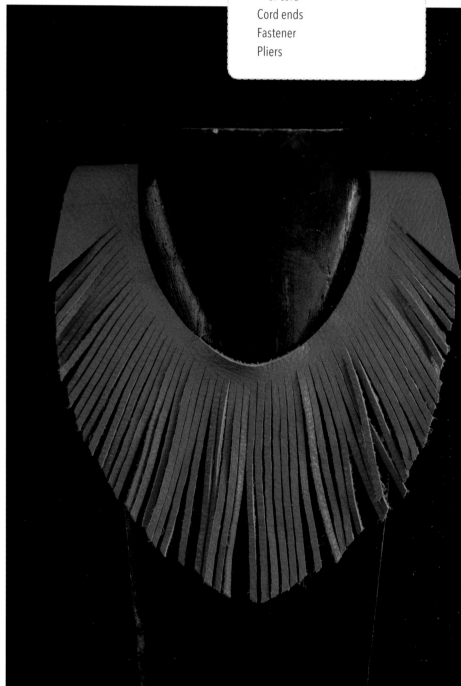

Earrings

XXXXXXXXXXXXXXXXXXXXXXXXXXXXXXXXXXXXXXXXXXXXXXXXXXXXXXXXXX

You will need

Dyed vegetable leather scraps
Templates on page 139
Cutting mat and cutting tools
Harness needle
Thread
Contact adhesive
Jump rings
Earring hooks
Pliers

1 Cut the leather into any shape or size you want, ensuring that the left and right sides are exact opposites. Use the patterns on page 139 if you don't want to do your own thing.

2 Punch the holes for the jump rings.

3 Decorate and embellish the earrings with stitches, by attaching other small pieces of leather or cutting fringes.

4 If you don't want the flesh side of the leather to show, die the backs of the earrings as well, or double up when you cut them and attach a mirror image lining once you have embellished them, using contact adhesive.

5 Attach a hook to the top of each earring using pliers and a jump ring.

HANGING PICTURE FRAMES

You will need

Vegetable leather dyed in the
    color of your choice
Templates on page 138
Cutting mat and cutting tools
Water-based dye
Felt and clothespin brush
2 harness needles
Thread
1 15 mm (³/₅ in.) O-ring
5 7 mm (¼ in.) rivets
Hammer and anvil

1 Prepare the templates according to the instructions on page 17.

2 Using the prepared templates, mark and cut out the leather, then stain the raw edges as explained on page 20, and punch all the stitching and rivet holes.

3 Place the front of the photo frame on the back, flesh sides together. The back of the photo frame doesn't have stitching holes all around. This forms the opening where you will insert the photo. Saddle stitch the front to the back, starting in the first stitching hole of the back panel, inserting the needle from the back, and work right around. When you get to the last hole in the back panel, push the needle between the two layers of leather and continue stitching the front panel only.

4 Once you get to the last hole, follow with the second needle to complete the saddle stitch and end off between the two layers of leather.

5 Repeat steps 3–4 for all the frames (2 squares, 2 rounds). You can also use cross-stitch.

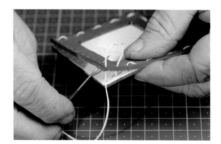

6 Slide the strap through the O-ring, fold the end over lining up the rivet holes and attach with a rivet.

7 Place each frame on the grain side of the strap with the rivet holes lining up and attach with a rivet. The openings for the photos should be at the top.

MAGAZINE RACK

⨯⨯

You will need

Vegetable leather dyed in the
  color of your choice
Template on page 131
Cutting mat and cutting tools
Water-based dye
Felt and peg brush
2 harness needles
Thread

1 Prepare the templates according to the instructions on page 17.

2 Using the prepared templates, mark and cut out the leather, then stain the raw edges as explained on page 20, and punch all the stitching holes. Don't be alarmed that the front and back panels are slightly longer than the base; it should be like that to prevent a raw edge from showing in the corner.

3 Place the right-hand side panel behind the front panel to form the corner, lining up the stitching holes. Starting at the top, cross-stitch (see page 25) down until you get to the bottom.

4 At the bottom, add the base to your layers and cross-stitch across the front panel of the box.

5 At the next corner, add the other side panel and sew up to the top. End off.

6 Go back to the bottom and, using a new piece of thread, sew the base to the side panel. At the next corner, add the back panel and sew up to the top of the corner. End off.

7 Go to the bottom and sew the back panel to the base; at the next corner, join the back and the first side panel, sewing up to the top of the corner and end off.

8 Go to the bottom and stitch the base to the side panel. End off.

9 Use a cross-stitch to decorate the top of the magazine rack.

10 Place the divider panels flesh sides together and join them by cross-stitching around the handle opening, then across the top.

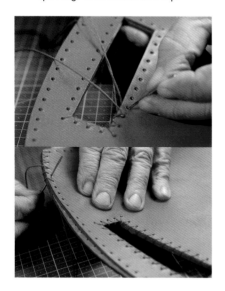

11 Thread your needles and thread through the bottom hole of the divider, then insert the divider. Starting from the inside and using a cross-stitch, sew the divider to the magazine rack. Start at the bottom and work your way up making sure that you stitch through the side panel as well as the divider. End off after each set of holes.

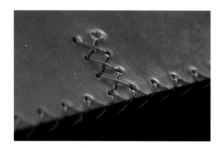 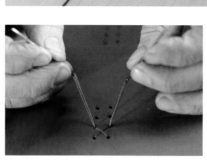 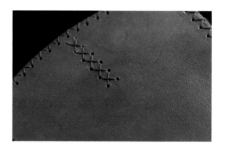

12 Repeat on the opposite side.

POUFFE

✕✕✕

You will need

Upholstery leather in two colors
Templates on page 160
Cutting mat and cutting tools
2 harness needles
2 sail needles
Thread
5 mm (⅛ in.) double-sided tape
50 cm (20 in.) zipper in a color
    matching the leather
Stuffing of your choice

1 Prepare the templates according to the instructions on page 17.

2 Using the prepared templates, mark and cut out the leather, punch the stitching holes, and cut out the zipper opening. For this project, we used cream and gray leather.

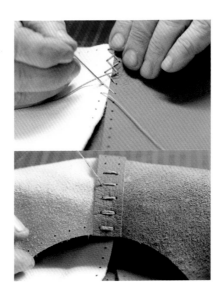

3 Place one gray and one cream side panel side to side, flesh side up, and the narrow top ends together.

4 Place a joint strip grain side up where the panels meet and join them by cross-stitching the joint strip to the panels starting from the very top holes. The cross-stitches are on the outside and the joint strip on the inside. Repeat until you have closed the circle with the last joint strip.

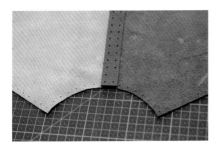

5 Turn the body flesh side out. Place the small circle inside the smaller top hole, grain sides together with at least two stitching holes lined up. Saddle stitch the circle to the body of the pouffe.

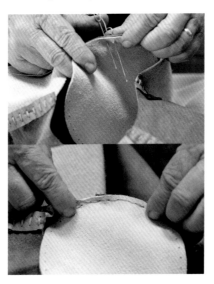

6 With the zipper facing up, adhere double-sided tape to both edges.

7 Place the bottom round panel of the pouffe flesh side up on your work surface. Adhere a small piece of double-sided tape to the end of the little flap inside the zipper opening. Fold the flap over backward and align the stitching holes. Temporarily stick the flap down to hold it in place. Repeat on the other side.

8 Remove the backing tape and glue the zipper over the opening, face side down.

9 Flip the panel over. Using the sail needles, make a double saddle stitch to secure one end of the zip, then saddle stitch to the other end, repeat the double stitch and saddle stitch along the other side back to where you began.

10 Open the zipper about 12 cm (4¾ in.). With the flesh side up, place the zipper panel in the big opening of the body panel with the zipper in the middle of one of the side panels. With the grain sides together, saddle stitch the zipper panel to the body.

11 Open the zip completely and turn the pouffe right side out.

12 Fill the pouffe with stuffing until it is the desired firmness.

FRINGED CUSHION COVER

XXXXXXXXXXXXXXXXXXXXXXXXXXXXXXXXXXXXXXXXXXXXXXXXXX

You will need

Suede leather
Templates on page 140
Cutting mat and cutting tools
2 harness needles
2 sail needles
Thread
45 cm (17¾ in.) zipper
45 x 45 cm (17¾ x 17¾ in.)
  cushion inner
5 mm (⅕ in.) double-sided
  tape

1 Prepare the templates according to the instructions on page 17.

2 Using the prepared templates, mark and cut out the leather, punch the stitching holes, cut out the zipper opening, and cut the fringes.

3 Place a fringe panel grain side up on the second row of stitching holes (second from the bottom) on the grain side of the front panel and saddle stitch in place.

4 Place another fringe panel on the third row of stitching holes and saddle stitch.

5 With the zipper facing up, adhere double-sided tape to both sides.

6 Remove the backing tape and glue the zipper over the zipper opening on the flesh side of the leather.

7 Turn the leather grain side up. Using the sail needles, start in the first hole of the row of stitching holes at the bottom of the zipper, make two stitches and then stitch up toward the stitching holes at the top of the zipper to secure the short end. Stitch back down and continue along the long side. At the other end, stitch up to secure the other short end. Follow with the second needle and end off at the opposite end from where you started.

8 Place the back and front panels flesh sides together with the fringes outside. Place the last fringe panel in position at the top of the cushion, lining up the stitching holes. Saddle stitch the three layers together, continuing right around the cushion to complete the cover. Start with the sail needles until the zipper has been incorporated, then switch to harness needles.

9 Open the zipper and insert the cushion inner.

BLANKET ROLL STRAP

×××

1 Prepare the templates according to the instructions on page 17.

2 Using the prepared templates, mark and cut out the leather, then stain the raw edges as explained on page 20, and punch all the stitching holes, buckle slots, and rivet holes.

3 Prepare the four loops by closing them with rivets (see page 22).

4 Take one closing strap and slide the end with the buckle slot through the half roller buckle until the prong fits through the buckle slot. Slide a completed loop in from the other end of the strap, up against the buckle.

5 Fold the short end of the strap over, lining up the rivet holes, trapping the loop between the two layers of the strap.

6 Place a buckle tab under the strap, lining up the rivet holes. Insert a rivet in the first hole closest to the loop and rivet the three layers together.

You will need

Vegetable leather dyed in the color of your choice
Templates on page 141
Cutting mat and cutting tools
Water-based dye
Felt and clothespin brush
2 harness needles
Thread
2 25 mm (1 in.) D-rings
2 25 mm (1 in.) metal rectangles
1 25 mm (1 in.) center prong roller buckle
2 25 mm (1 in.) harness buckles (half buckle)
12 8 mm (1/3 in.) rivets
Hammer and anvil

7 Slide a second loop in from the other end of the strap. Push it right up against the rivet, between the two layers of leather.

8 Insert a rivet into the remaining hole and rivet the two layers together.

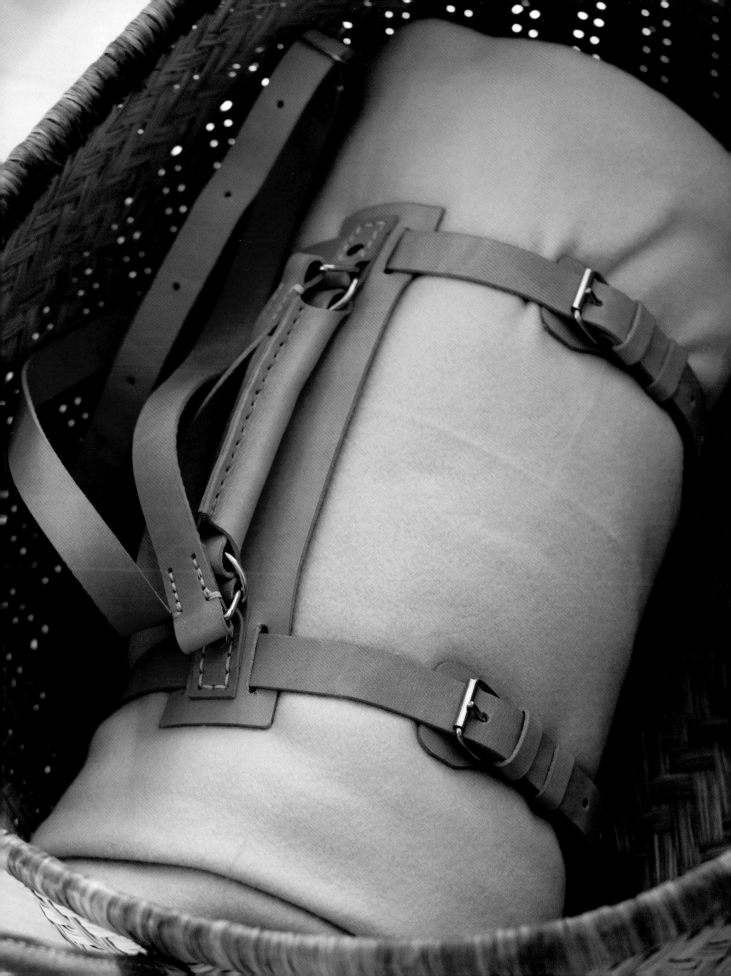

9 Repeat with the other closing strap.

10 Slide one flap of the handle through the D-ring (straight side of the D-ring facing out) and fold over the flap. Place the handle inner grain side up over the flap end, lining up the rivet holes, and secure with the rivet.

11 Repeat on the other side of the handle.

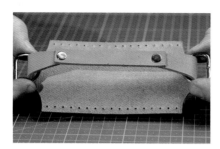

12 Close the handle and saddle stitch the two layers together, starting and ending with a side stitch.

13 Slide a handle tab through the handle D-ring, folding over the end with fewer stitching holes. Slide in the metal rectangle as well so that it lies on top of the D-ring.

14 Close the tab, lining up the rivet holes. Place the handle tab on top of the handle base, grain side up, lining up the rivet holes of all three layers. Secure with a rivet and saddle stitch, then repeat on the other side.

15 Slide the buckle strap (buckle slot end) through the roller buckle until the prong fits through the buckle slot. Fold over the end and line up the stitching holes. Starting at the hole closest to the buckle, make a side stitch and stitch down to the end of the row. Sew back up to form the saddle stitch and end off, then repeat on the other side.

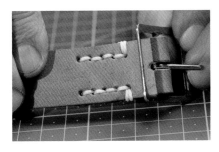

16 Slide the other end of the strap through the metal rectangle of the handle tab, fold over, and secure with saddle stitch in the same way as step 15.

17 Slide the sling-strap end with the stitching holes through the metal rectangle on the other side of the handle. Fold over and secure with saddle stitch in the same way.

18 Thread the closing straps that you prepared earlier through the slots on the handle base.

MAGIC SANDAL

1 Prepare the templates according to the instructions on page 17.

2 Using the prepared templates, mark and cut out the leather and EVA rubber soles. Cut the straps with a strap cutter (see page 11) if you have access to one, otherwise cut them by hand. Stain the raw edges as explained on page 20, and punch all the rivet holes and buckle slots.

3 Use a skiving tool or an NT cutter to skive off the ends of the back straps and the buckle ends of the long straps.

4 Using an edge beveler, remove the sharp edges of the straps (on the inside of the leather) so that they won't chafe your feet.

PREPARING THE SOLES

5 Do both shoes at the same time. Using sandpaper, slightly roughen the smooth side of the rubber sole and heel.

6 Place the smooth side of the heel against the rough side of the sole and mark the position with a pencil.

7 Use sandpaper to smooth the rough side of the sole where the heel will be glued on (the area that you have just marked).

8   Apply adhesive to both the heel and the sole, set aside to dry until tacky, and then attach the heel to the sole. Hit the sole with a rubber mallet to apply enough pressure to secure it in place.

Preparing the insoles and straps

9   Using sandpaper, slightly roughen the flesh side of the insole so that the glue can penetrate the leather.

11   Fold over the ends of the strap (to the inside), lining up the rivet holes, and attach rivets to secure. The thinner, skived ends will ensure that there is no chafing.

10   Thread the back strap through the back slots of the insole (marked 1 and 2 on the pattern) with the flesh side facing in.

12   Slide the buckle end of the long strap through the roller buckle until the prong fits through the buckle slot. Fold over the strap, lining up the rivet holes, and secure with a rivet.

Assembling the Sandal

13 Insert the long strap from front to back through the loop of the back strap on the outer side of the sole, pulling it through until the buckle meets the back strap. Bring round the long strap and insert it from back to front through the other back strap. Take it across the sole to slot 3 and push it through to the back, then up again through slot 4. Take it to slot 5, pushing it through the slot to the bottom, and up again through slot 6.

14 Place your foot in the sandal and feed the strap from the buckle end, pulling on the other end until it fits snugly around your foot and toe. Close the buckle and mark the buckle hole used so that you can remove your foot and close the buckle in the same position again.

15 Turn over the shoe and mark the position of the foot and toe straps in pen. Apply glue to the bottom of the insole avoiding the areas of the two front straps as these need to be adjusted to fit snugly over your foot.

16 Apply glue to the smooth side of the rubber sole. Spread Vaseline on the two front straps so that they can slide easily once the sole is glued on.

17 When the glue is dry enough, place the insole on top of the sole and use a rubber mallet to apply pressure and firm it down, especially on the outside of the straps. Open the buckle if necessary.

18 Pull on the front strap to ensure that it moves easily and is not glued down.

19 Use sandpaper to smooth the edges of the sandal.

CASUAL BELT

✕✕✕

You will need

Vegetable leather dyed in the
    color of your choice
Templates on page 148
Cutting mat and cutting tools
Strap cutter
Water-based dye
Felt and clothespin brush
Skiving tool
2 harness needles
Thread
35 mm (1⅜ in.) half buckle

1   Prepare the templates according to the instructions on page 17.

2   Using the prepared template, mark and cut out the belt, adjusting the length as required. Use a strap cutter (see page 11) if you have access to one, otherwise cut by hand. Stain the raw edges as explained on page 20, and punch all the stitching and adjusting holes and the buckle slot.

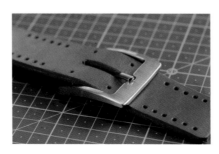

3   Use a skiving tool or an NT cutter to skive off the buckle end of the belt to make it thinner (on the flesh side).

4   Place the belt loop ends flush against each other and close with a cross-stitch.

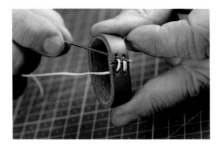

5   Slide the belt into the buckle until the prong fits through the buckle slot.

6   Fold over the end and line up the stitching holes. Make a side stitch just under the bar of the buckle on both sides and slide in the loop from the other end.

7   Push the loop all the way to the buckle bar. Start with the stitching hole furthest from the loop and insert the needle between the two layers of leather. Saddle stitch up toward the loop and make a double

side stitch just under the loop. Work back to the start and finish off by inserting the needle between the two layers and knotting the ends. The knot should be between the two layers and not visible.

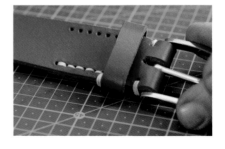

8   Repeat on the other side.

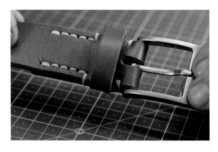

CURVED LADIES' BELT

You will need

Side leather
Template on page 149
Cutting mat and cutting tools
Revolving punch
1 holster stud
Screwdriver

1   Prepare the template according to the instructions on page 17.

2   Using the prepared template, mark and cut out the belt, adjusting the length as required. Punch the adjusting holes and the hole for the holster stud using a revolving punch.

3   Cut the slits where the adjusting holes are.

4   Attach the holster stud by fastening the screw at the bottom.

STUDDED THREE-STRING LADIES' BELT

XXXXXXXXXXXXXXXXXXXXXXXXXXXXXXXXXXXXXXXXXX

You will need

Vegetable leather dyed in the
    color of your choice
Templates on page 148
Cutting mat and cutting tools
Strap cutter
Water-based dye
Felt and clothespin brush
105 7 mm (¼ in.) rivets
    (depending on the length of
    your belt—we made a 80 cm
    / 31½ in. belt)
25 mm (1 in.) half buckle
2 32 mm (1¼ in.) O-ring
Hammer and anvil

1 Prepare the templates according to
the instructions on page 17.

2 Using the prepared templates,
mark and cut out the belt, adjusting
the length as required. Stain the
raw edges as explained on page 20,
and punch the rivet and adjusting
holes and the buckle slot.

3 Start with three center straps. Fold
the ends over the O-rings, lining
up the rivet holes, and secure
with rivets.

4 Attach rivets in the remaining holes
on the straps.

5   Prepare the belt loop by closing it
    with a rivet.

6   Slide the buckle end into the
    buckle until the prong fits through
    the buckle slot (prong toward the
    short end).

7   Fold over the end, lining up the
    rivet holes, and secure the buckle
    with two rivets.

8   Slide the loop in from the other
    end, placing it between the two
    layers, and attach two rivets just
    under the loop.

9   Slide the other end through the
    other side of the O-ring, fold over
    until the rivet holes line up and
    secure with two rivets.

10 Slide the belt end through the
    other end of the other O-ring (the
    end where the two rivet holes are),
    fold over the leather and secure
    with two rivets.

MEN'S WALLET

You will need

Upholstery leather
Templates on page 150
Cutting mat and cutting tools
2 harness needles
Thread
2 press studs
Press-stud tool
Mallet

1   Prepare the templates according to the instructions on page 17.

2   Using the prepared templates, mark and cut out the leather and punch the stitching and rivet holes.

3   Align the stitching holes of the closing tab with the relevant ones on the outer body, both grain sides up, and attach it using a saddle stitch (see page 24).

4   Attach the cap of the press stud to the end of the closing tab so that the socket is on the flesh side of the leather (see page 22).

Then attach the bottom of the press stud to the outer body where the rivet hole is, with the post of the press stud on the grain side of the leather.

5   Attach the cap top of the press stud to the coin purse flap with the socket on the flesh side of the leather, and attach the bottom to the coin purse front with the stud on the grain side.

6   Align one of the credit card holder inserts with the top short row of stitching holes on the credit card holder base, both grain sides up. Saddle stitch along the short row, then repeat with the other insert on the bottom short row.

7   Place the credit card holder front on top, grain side up. Lining up the stitching holes with the bottom row of stitching holes on the base, saddle stitch only the right-hand side for now.

8   Place the coin purse gusset on the right-hand side edge of the coin purse front, flesh sides together. Starting at the top, sew the gusset to the coin purse front to the last hole on the gusset (don't include the last hole on the front panel). End off.

9   Place the coin purse front with the gusset attached on the coin purse base, flesh sides together, so that the gusset stitching holes on the other side line up with those on the coin purse base, leaving open two holes at the top. (Make a fold in the gusset to be able to attach it correctly to the base.) Starting at the bottom hole, sew to the top of the gusset using a saddle stitch. Do not end off.

10   Place the coin purse flap on the right-hand side of the inner body with the stitching holes lining up with the stitching holes on the body. Place the coin purse base and front with gusset over the coin purse flap and continue with your saddle stitching through all three layers of leather to the end of the row. End off.

11   Place the credit card base with the loose front on the left-hand side of the inner body, flesh sides together. Make one stitch at the top right-hand side to hold the credit card base in place.

12   Place the outer body flesh side up on your work surface with the closing tab to your right. Place the upper lining grain side up on the outer body's top row of stitching holes and saddle stitch the top row only.

13   Aligning the bottom edges, place the inner body with coin purse and credit card holder on top of the

outer body. Using a saddle stitch and starting at the bottom of the coin purse where the stitching holes in the outer body begin, sew through all the layers to the top of the upper lining and end off.

14   Return to the stitching holes at the bottom where the credit card holder is aligned and stitch around the other side through all the layers to the top of the upper lining.

15   Whipstitch around the outer edge if you wish to use a decorative stitch.

NOTE: There is more space between the bottom stitching holes in the outer body than on the inner body. This is correct and you need to align the stitching holes, not the gaps between. This is to allow for the wallet to be filled with bills and folded.

LADIES' PURSE

XXXXXXXXXXXXXXXXXXXXXXXXXXXXXXXXXXXXXXXXXXXXXXXXXXXXXX

You will need

Upholstery leather
Templates on page 151
Cutting mat and cutting tools
2 harness needles
2 sail needles
Thread
1 press stud
Press-stud tool
20 cm (7⅞ in.) zipper
5 mm (⅕ in.) double-sided
    tape
Mallet

1 Prepare the templates according to the instructions on page 17.

2 Using the prepared templates, mark and cut out the leather, including the zipper opening, and punch the stitching and rivet holes.

3 With the zipper facing up, adhere double-sided tape to both sides. Remove the backing tape and glue the zipper facedown into the opening of the zipper pocket (on the flesh side).

4 Using the sail needles, saddle stitch (see page 24) right around the zipper to attach it to the pocket.

5 With the grain sides up, line up the bottom stitching holes of a credit card holder insert with the first short row of stitching holes on the credit card holder base and saddle stitch. Repeat with the other three inserts, using the remaining short rows of stitching holes.

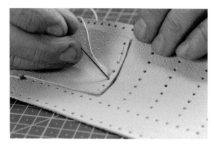

6 Align the bottom stitching holes of the credit card holder front with the next row of stitching holes on the base. Starting in the top right-hand corner, saddle stitch the inserts and front to the base.

7 Place the gusset on the base, flesh sides together. Starting in one corner with a double overstitch, saddle stitch the gusset to the base, shaping the gusset around the curves. Set aside the assembled credit card base.

8 Attach the bottom of the press stud (see page 22) in the rivet hole on the outer body with the post on the grain side. Attach the top of the press stud to the closing tab with the socket on the flesh side of the leather.

9 Place the closing tab in position on the opposite end of the outer body, both grain side up, and attach it using a saddle stitch.

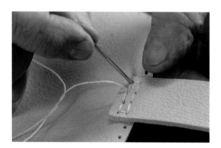

10 Fold the zipper pocket over, flesh sides together, and place it on the flesh side of the outer body, with the zipper in the middle, on the side where the closing tab is. Leaving one stitching hole open on both sides at the top (for the overstitch), start (and end) with an overstitch and saddle stitch the zipper pocket to the outer body.

11 Attach the assembled credit card base to the outer body on the opposite side of the zip pocket. Place the gusset and the outer body flesh sides together and line up the stitching holes, leaving one stitching hole open on both sides at the top. Starting (and ending) with an overstitch, saddle stitch the gusset to the outer body.

12 Finish the outer edge with a whipstitch (see page 25). This is decorative and therefore optional.

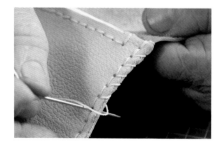

FRINGED SLING BAG

1 Prepare the templates according to the instructions on page 17.

2 Using the prepared templates, mark and cut out the leather, including the zipper opening, and punch the buckle slots and the stitching, rivet, and adjusting holes.

3 Place the bag body flesh side up on your work surface. Fold back the small flaps inside the zipper opening, lining up the flap stitching hole with the matching stitching hole on the bag. Secure the flap to the body with two side stitches on either side.

4 With the zipper facing up, apply double-sided tape on both sides. Remove the backing tape and glue the zipper facedown into the zipper opening.

5 Turn the body grain side up. Using a saddle stitch and the sail needles, start on the edge of the bag and sew the zipper to the bag. When you reach the fourth hole, stitch up to the top row of holes and back again to secure the zipper end.

6 Continue sewing along the bottom row of stitching holes until you reach the fourth last hole. Stitch up to the top row of holes and back again to secure the zipper end. Continue stitching to the edge of the bag. End off.

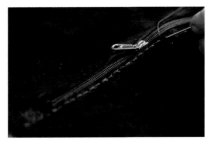

7 Align the fringed panel, grain side up, with the row of stitching holes on the other side of the zipper. Leaving open one hole on either side of the fringed panel, saddle stitch through the two layers of suede and the zipper, starting and ending with a side stitch.

You will need

Suede leather
Matching vegetable leather for the sling strap
Templates on page 144
Cutting mat and cutting tools
2 harness needles
2 sail needles
Thread
1 15 mm (3/5 in.) roller buckle
1 25 cm (1 in.) zipper
2 15 mm (3/5 in.) trigger hooks
3 6 mm (1/4 in.) rivets
5 mm (1/5 in.) double-sided tape
27 cm (10 2/3 in.) zipper
Hammer and anvil

8 Open the zipper slightly, then fold the bag over with the zipper in the middle and the fringe between the two outer layers of suede. Align the stitching holes around the edge of the bag and saddle stitch right around the bag to the other end of the zipper.

9 Turn the bag the right side out.

Preparing the Sling

10 Slide the buckle strap into the buckle until the prong fits through the buckle slot. Fold over the end of the strap and secure with a rivet (see page 22).

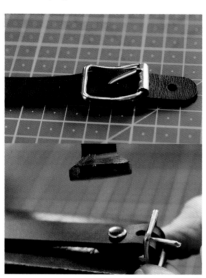

11 Slide the other end of the strap through the snap hook, fold over the end and secure with a rivet. Attach a snap hook to the sling strap in the same way.

12 Hook the snap hooks into the loops on either side of the zipper and fasten the buckle using the adjusting holes to adjust the length of the sling.

OVERNIGHT BAG

✕✕

You will need

Side leather
Templates on page 147
Cutting mat and cutting tools
2 harness needles
2 sail needles
Thread
1 55 cm (21²/₃ in.) zipper
2 35 cm (13²/₅ in.) sash cord
   (8 mm/¹/₃ in.)
Contact adhesive
5 mm (¹/₅ in.) double-sided
   tape
Base inner of 15 x 45 cm
   (5⁹/₁₀ x 17⁷/₁₀ in.)
Pen

1 Prepare the templates according to the instructions on page 17.

2 Using the prepared templates, mark and cut out the leather, including the zipper opening, and punch the stitching holes.

3 Apply contact adhesive to the flesh side of the handles between the inner rows of stitching holes.

Allow to dry, then place the sash cord in the middle of the glued area and fold over the handle. Apply pressure with your fingers to adhere the two sides. Saddle stitch along the stitching holes, starting and ending with an overstitch.

4 Place one end of a handle on the back panel, both grain sides up, and align the stitching holes. Place a handle tab on the inside of the back panel, skin sides together so that you now have three aligning layers.

5 Saddle stitch the handle to the bag, starting and ending with a double stitch. Repeat with the other end of the handle and follow the same steps to secure the second handle to the bag front.

6 With the zipper faceup, adhere double-sided tape to both sides. Remove the backing tape and place it facedown over the zipper opening on the flesh side of the zipper gusset. Saddle stitch right around the zipper.

7 Place the base in the center of the bottom gusset, flesh sides together, and trace the outline with a pen. Apply contact adhesive to this area and to the flesh side of the base. Once the glue is tacky, adhere the base to the gusset by applying pressure with your hands to secure it in place.

8 Place the short side of the zipper gusset over the short side of the bottom gusset, both grain sides up. Place the zipper tab on top, lining up both rows of stitching holes with the zipper tab exactly in the middle.

9 Start at the closest edge of the zipper tab and saddle stitch right around the two rows of stitching holes to secure the zipper tab and the gussets. Repeat on the other side.

10 Turn the gusset panel inside out. Lining up the center notches, place the front panel on the gusset, grain sides together. Start in the middle and saddle stitch the front panel to the gusset, lining up the stitching holes and working right around back to where you started.

11 Attach the back panel in the same way, leaving the zipper slightly open so that you can turn the bag right side out once you have completed your stitching.

12 Turn the bag grain side out, using your fingers to flatten and shape the seam on the inside.

13 Insert the base inner.

POSTMAN'S SLING

XXXXXXXXXXXXXXXXXXXXXXXXXXXXXXXXXXXXXXXXXXXXX

1 Prepare the templates according to the instructions on page 17.

2 Using the prepared templates, mark and cut out the leather, including the zipper opening, and punch the buckle slot and stitching and rivet holes.

3 With the zipper faceup, adhere double-sided tape to both sides. Remove the backing tape and place the zipper facedown over the zipper opening on the flesh side of the pocket. Saddle stitch right around the zipper.

4 Fold over the top edge of the pen holder pocket, flesh sides together, line up the two rows of stitching holes and saddle stitch across.

5 Place the pen holder pocket on the zipper pocket, both grain side up. Join by saddle stitching along the two vertical rows of stitching holes in the middle. Start at the bottom and end off each row.

6 Place the zipper pocket on its backing, flesh sides together. Starting in one of the top corners, saddle stitch down, then right around to the other top corner (don't sew the top edge yet).

7 Place the back top lining over the top edge of the pocket (grain side up), lining up its bottom row of stitching holes with the pocket stitching holes. Leave four holes open on one side and five on the other side. Starting at the edge of the back top lining, saddle stitch across the bottom row to the other edge.

You will need

Side leather
Templates on page 146
Cutting mat and cutting tools
2 harness needles
2 sail needles
Thread
25 cm (10 in.) zipper
5 mm (1/5 in.) double-sided tape
30 mm (1 1/5 in.) roller buckle
1 8 mm (1/3 in.) rivet
Hammer and anvil

8 Place the side top lining on the top (narrow) edge of the gusset, flesh sides together, and saddle stitch. Repeat with the other side gusset.

9 Place the bottom (wider) edge of the side gusset over the bottom gusset, both grain sides up. Saddle stitch between the two slits, leaving open one hole on either side, starting and ending with an overstitch. Repeat with the other side gusset.

10 Slide the buckle strap into the buckle until the prong fits through the buckle slot. Fold the buckle end over and secure it with a rivet just below the prong.

11 With both grain sides up, place the buckle strap on the side gusset where the stitching holes are. Saddle stitch the strap to the gusset, making a double row of stitches at the top.

12 Attach the sling strap to the other side gusset in the same way.

13 Place the top front lining on the top (narrower) edge of the front panel, flesh sides together, and saddle stitch across the top edge.

14 Place the back panel grain side up on your work surface. Place the flap on the back edge, also grain side up, aligning the flap stitching holes with the second row of stitching holes on the back panel. Saddle stitch across.

15 Turn the back panel and flap over, flesh side up. Place the zipper pocket on the back panel, lining up the top row of stitching holes on the top lining with the top row of stitching holes on the back panel. Saddle stitch across the top (don't sew down the short sides yet).

16 Make a fold line with your fingers along the long sides of the gusset, grain side up.

17 Place the gusset on the front panel, flesh sides together. Starting at the top where the front top lining is, make an overstitch and then saddle stitch down the side, across the bottom and up the other side, ending with an overstitch. The slits in the gusset create the corners of the sling bag.

18 Place the gusset on the back panel, flesh sides together, with the top back lining at the top. Saddle stitch the back panel to the gusset in the same way, starting and ending with an overstitch.

BASKET

XXXXXXXXXXXXXXXXXXXXXXXXXXXXXXXXXXXXXXXX

You will need

Vegetable leather dyed in the
    color of your choice
Templates on page 145
Cutting mat and cutting tools
Water-based dye
Felt and clothespin brush
2 harness needles
Thread

1 Prepare the templates according to the instructions on page 17.

2 Using the prepared templates, mark and cut out the leather, then stain the raw edges as explained on page 20, and punch all the stitching holes.

3 Place a front tab filler on the front panel where the stitching holes are and place the front tab on top (all grain side up). Saddle stitch a rectangle and finish with a cross inside the rectangle. Repeat on the other side of the tab.

4 Place the flap tip filler on the flap where the matching stitching holes are, with the flap tip on top (all grain side up). Saddle stitch around the rectangle. Make a double row of stitches where the flap will hook to strengthen the tab.

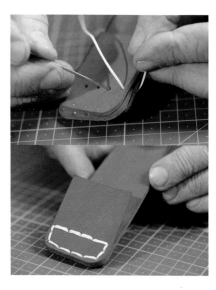

5 Place the prepared flap grain side up on the grain side of the back panel with the long side of the flap hanging over the edge. Saddle stitch the flap to the back, connecting all the holes so that they form four smaller squares.

6 Lay out the two middle panels on your work surface so that you can see how the closing mechanism will work.

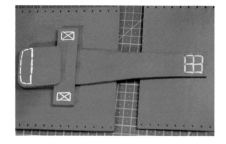

110

7 Place the front and one side panel flesh side up against each other. Place the joining strap grain side up over the seam, lining up the top holes so that the bottom row remains open. Starting at the top, begin with a double stitch and cross-stitch the joining strap to the two panels, including the bottom row. The crosses are on the outside (grain side) of the panels. End off.

8 Attach the back panel to the other side of the side panel in the same way, then attach the remaining side panel to the back panel.

9 Fold the front and side panel toward each other so that the edges are flush against each other (grain side out). Place the joining strip on the inside and cross-stitch the panels together. You will now stitch from the outside of the basket so make sure that the crosses are on the right side.

10 Dampen the edge of the base and, with the grain side up, fold over the edge all around with your fingers.

11 Insert the base into the bottom of the basket, lining up the center of the base with the center of the back panel. With the flesh sides together, saddle stitch all the way around.

12 Place the handle on the stitching holes at the top of the basket and saddle stitch around the rectangle making a double row of stitches at the top. Repeat on the other side and with the other handle.

LUGGAGE TAG

You will need

Side leather
Templates on page 152
Cutting mat and cutting tools
2 harness needles
Thread
A4 heavy-duty plastic or
    acetate film
13 mm (½ in.) roller buckle
1 7 mm (¼ in.) rivet
Hammer and anvil

1 Prepare the templates according to the instructions on page 17.

2 Using the prepared templates, mark and cut out the leather and plastic or acetate window, and punch the stitching and rivet holes as well as the buckle and strap slots.

3 Slide the end of the strap through the buckle until the prong fits through the buckle slot (prong facing toward the short end of the strap). Fold over the end and secure with a rivet.

4 Place the back panel flesh side up on your work surface. Adhere double-sided tape to the two long sides on the inside of the stitching holes.

5 Glue the plastic window on top, lining up the strap slots.

6 Place the front window on the back and plastic (flesh sides together), lining up all the stitching holes. Join the three layers using any stitch you prefer.

7 Slide the strap through the strap slot and close the strap with the buckle.

TABLET COVER

You will need

Upholstery leather (scraps in a contrasting color)
Templates on page 127
Cutting mat and cutting tools
2 harness needles
Thread
1 9 mm (⅜ in.) rivet
1 7 mm (¼ in.) rivet
Hammer and anvil

1 Prepare the templates according to the instructions on page 17.

2 Using the prepared templates, mark and cut out the leather and the button thong, and punch the stitching and rivet holes.

3 Place the button spacer on the grain side of the front panel (where the rivet hole is) with the button on top. Secure with a rivet.

4 Attach the button thong to the flap by placing the button spacer on the flesh side and the thong on the grain side of the flap where the rivet hole is. Secure with a rivet.

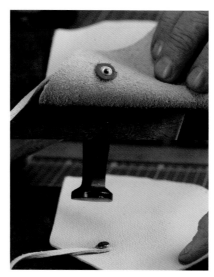

5 Place the flap on the back panel where the stitching holes are away from the edge, both grain side up. Saddle stitch the two layers together.

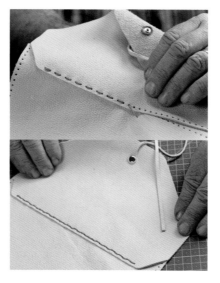

6 Flip the back and flap over and place the front in position on the back panel, flesh sides together with the stitching holes aligned. Saddle stitch together along three sides, beginning and ending with a side stitch.

114

PEN HOLDER

You will need

Vegetable leather dyed in the color of your choice
Templates on page 153
Cutting mat and cutting tools
Water-based dye
Felt and clothespin brush
2 harness needles
Thread
1 m (39⅜ in.) cord

1 Prepare the templates according to the instructions on page 17.

2 Using the prepared templates, mark and cut out the leather, including the opening, then stain the raw edges as explained on page 20, and punch all the stitching and cord holes.

3 Place the two panels flesh sides together. Start at the top and saddle stitch the panels together. You can also use a cross-stitch.

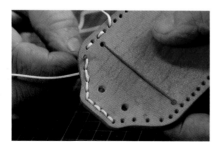

4 Slide the cord through the cord holes and knot at the back.

ASSORTED KEY RINGS

You will need

Leather scraps
Templates on page 153
Cutting mat and cutting tools
Key rings
Rivets
Hammer and anvil

Making key rings is the ideal way to get rid of small scraps of leather—you can use any kind. Cut the leather according to the templates on page 153. Where there is only one hole, use it for the key ring. Where there are two holes, slide the end through the key ring, fold over and attach with a rivet.

TASSEL KEY RING

You will need

Upholstery leather
Template on page 153
Cutting mat and cutting tools
Revolving punch
Key ring
10 mm (²/₅ in.) double-cap rivet
10 mm (²/₅ in.) double-sided
    tape
Hammer and anvil

1 Prepare the template according to the instructions on page 17.

2 Using the prepared template, mark and cut out the leather.

3 Adhere double-sided tape to the solid edge of the fringe (flesh side).

4 Remove the backing tape. Form a loop with the wide fringe on the right-hand side, grain side out, pressing it down onto the tape after slipping in a key ring.

5 Pushing down firmly, fold the fringe over onto itself (grain to flesh) repeatedly, keeping it glued down with the adhesive tape.

6 Punch a hole through all the layers and attach with a rivet.

118

SNAP HOOK KEY RING

1 Prepare the template according to the instructions on page 17.

2 Using the prepared template, mark and cut out the leather, then stain the raw edges as explained on page 20, and punch the rivet holes.

3 Slide the narrow end through the snap hook, fold over the edge and line up the rivet holes.

4 Turn it over, fold over the bottom of the strap and line up the rivet hole with the narrow end in the middle. Secure with a double-cap rivet and attach a key ring to the snap hook.

You will need

Vegetable leather dyed in the color of your choice
Templates on page 152
Cutting mat and cutting tools
Water-based dye
Felt and clothespin brush
9 mm (⅜ in.) double-cap rivet
13 mm (½ in.) snap hook
Key ring
Hammer and anvil

COASTER SET

You will need

Vegetable leather dyed in the
   color of your choice
Templates on page 152
Cutting mat and cutting tools
Water-based dye
Felt and clothespin brush
Holster stud
Srewdriver
4 8 mm (¹/₃ in.) rivets
Hammer and anvil

1 Prepare the templates according to the instructions on page 17.

2 Using the prepared templates, mark and cut out the leather, then stain the raw edges as explained on page 20, and punch the rivet holes. Cut the holster stud slit.

3 Attach the holster stud in the center hole on the narrow end of the strap—the screw should be on the flesh side.

4 Place the same end of the strap on the middle of the holding band, both grain side up. Line up the rivet holes and secure with rivets.

5 Flip over the band and strap that you have just assembled. Fold the narrow end of the holding band over, lining up the rivet hole with the first hole in the center of the strap, and secure with a rivet.

6 Repeat on the other side with the two narrow ends of the holding band now flush in the center of the strap.

7 Insert the coasters into the pocket that you've created. Close by pushing the stud hole in the strap over the holster stud.

CANDLE HOLDER

You will need

Vegetable leather dyed in the color of your choice
Templates on page 125
Cutting mat and cutting tools
Water-based dye
Felt and clothespin brush
1 10 mm (²/₅ in.) rivet
Hammer and anvil

1 Prepare the templates according to the instructions on page 17.

2 Using the prepared templates, mark and cut out the leather, then stain the raw edges as explained on page 20, and punch the rivet holes.

3 Place the spacer on the body, both grain side up, lining it up with the rivet hole at the bottom in the center, with the button on top of the spacer.

4 Secure with a rivet.

5 With the body flesh side up, fold over the bottom flap and fold in the flaps on either side of the button, as shown below and indicated on the pattern with dotted lines.

6 Make a knot in the thong and lace the thong through the bottom of the center holes on the body (from the back). Fold over one long side flap of the body and lace the thong through the bottom hole and repeat with the other side flap, creating the candle pocket.

7 Fold the bottom of the body up and fold in the short flap. Lace the thong through the bottom hole. Fold over the other short flap and lace the thong through the bottom hole.

8 Lace the thong through the top holes of the pocket (from the inside). Add the tie grain side up and lace the thong through the hole.

9   Lace the thong through the remaining three holes on the body, in and out until you reach the top (go through all the layers of leather so that the thong emerges at the back).

10 Make sure that you pull the thong tight while you lace. Make a knot to secure the thong and cut off the excess (1 cm [2/5 in.] from the knot). Fasten the tie by wrapping it around the button.

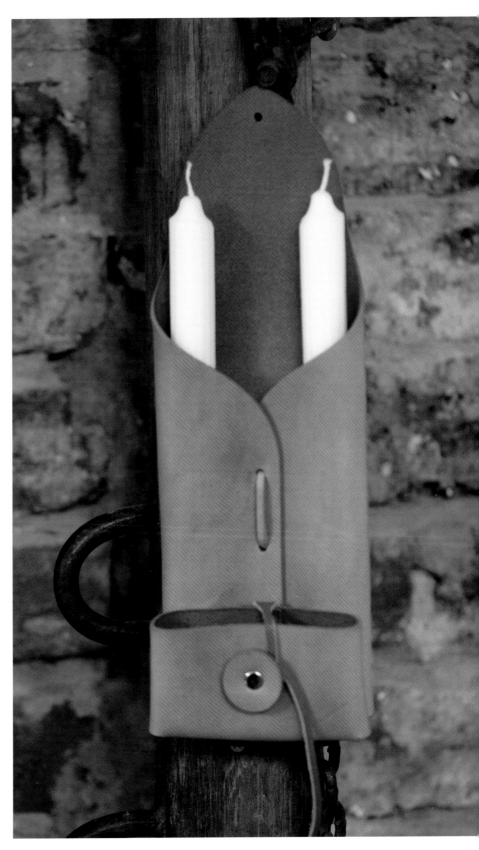

TEMPLATES

Fringed neckpiece
Scale 1:3

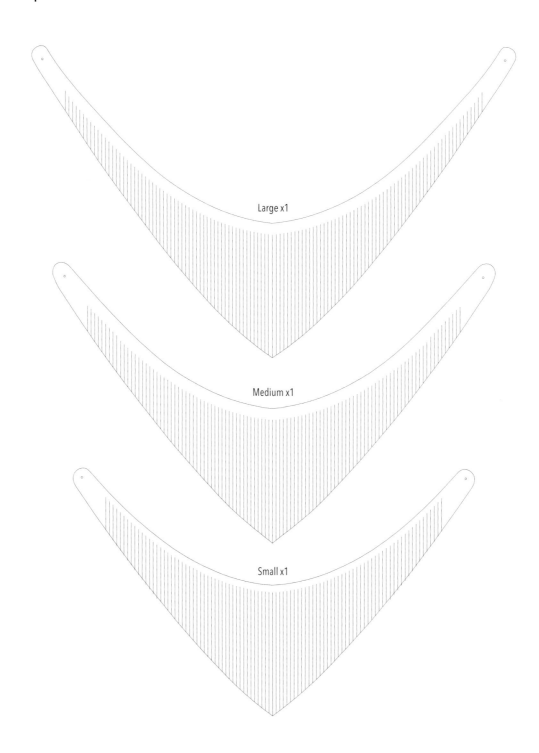

Large x1

Medium x1

Small x1

Candle holder
Scale 1:2

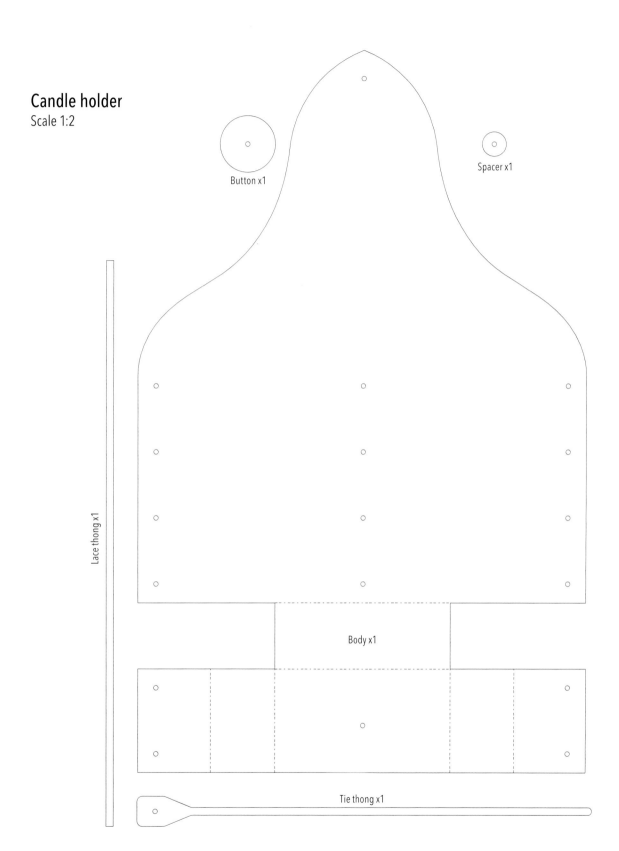

Button x1

Spacer x1

Lace thong x1

Body x1

Tie thong x1

Backpack
Scale 1:5

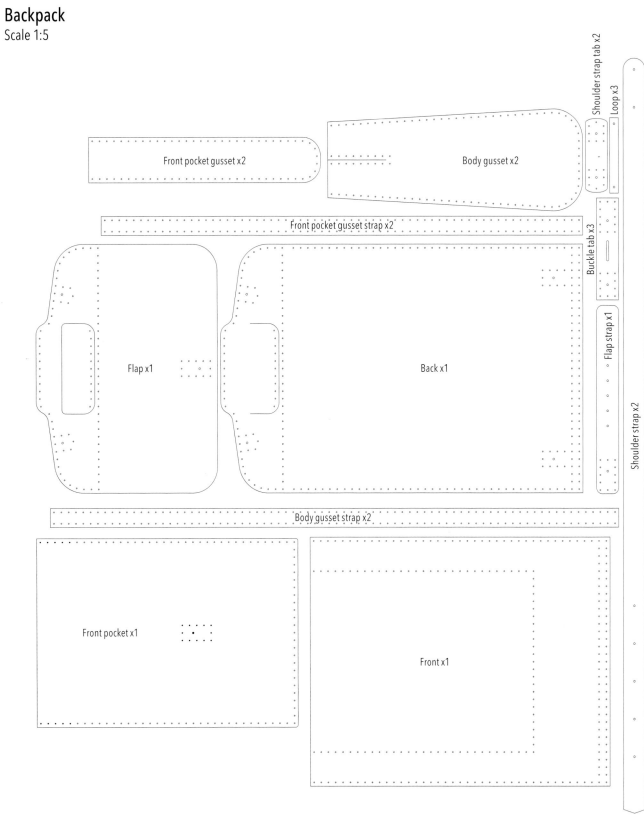

Tablet cover
Scale 1:3

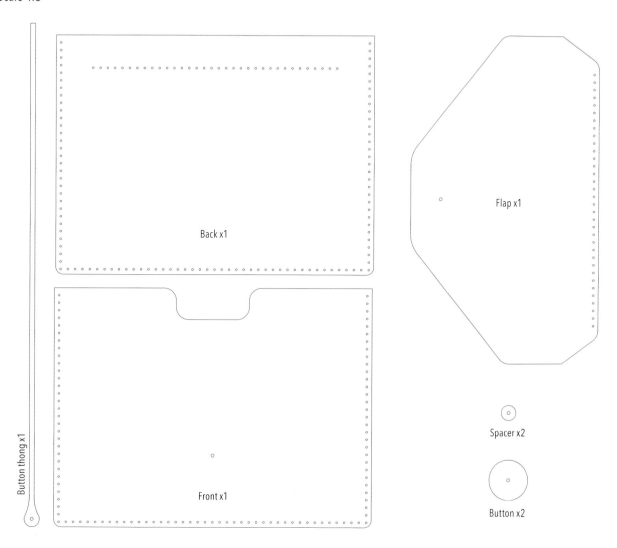

Button thong x1

Back x1

Front x1

Flap x1

Spacer x2

Button x2

12-string armband
Scale 1:2

Adjust to required length*

*Suggested final length:
Large = 225 mm (8⁴/₅ in.)
Medium = 215 mm (8²/₅ in.)
Small = 195 mm (7³/₅ in.)

In-box
Scale 1:3

Side x2

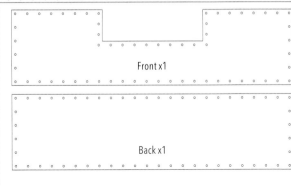

Front x1

Back x1

Base x1

Small bin
Scale 1:4

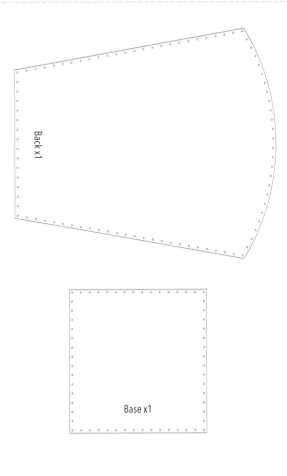

Front x1

Back x1

Side x2

Base x1

A4 document holder

Scale 1:4

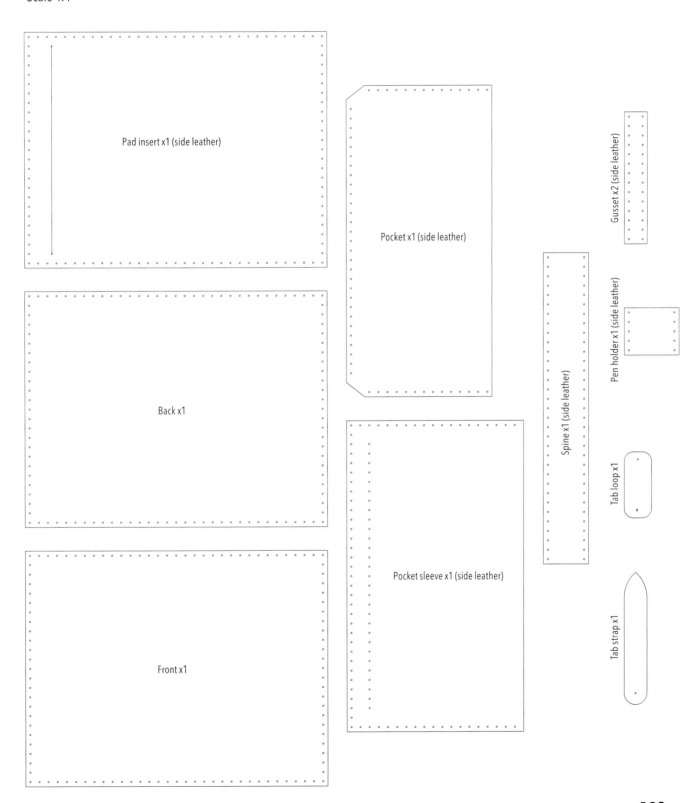

Pad insert x1 (side leather)

Pocket x1 (side leather)

Gusset x2 (side leather)

Back x1

Pen holder x1 (side leather)

Spine x1 (side leather)

Tab loop x1

Front x1

Pocket sleeve x1 (side leather)

Tab strap x1

Desk blotter
Scale 1:3

Base x1

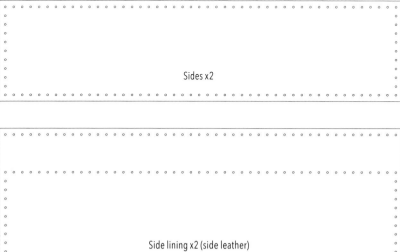

Sides x2

Side lining x2 (side leather)

Pencil bag
Scale 1:2

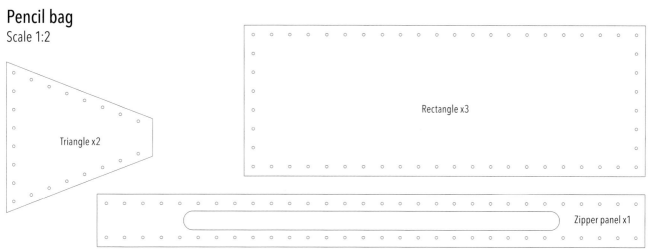

Triangle x2

Rectangle x3

Zipper panel x1

Magazine rack
Scale 1:5

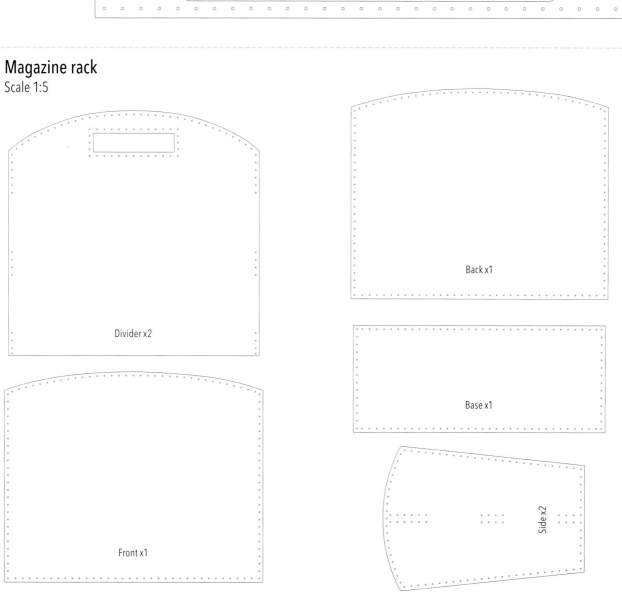

Divider x2

Back x1

Base x1

Front x1

Side x2

Firewood carrier
Scale 1:4

Base x1

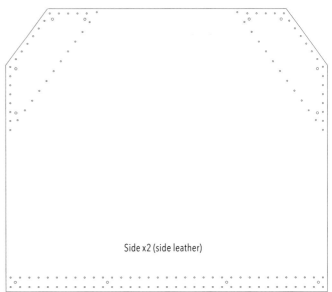

Side x2 (side leather)

Handle x2

Dice cup
Scale 1:2

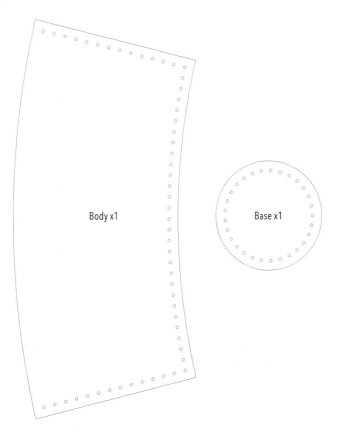

Body x1

Base x1

Two-bottle wine carrier
Scale 1:3

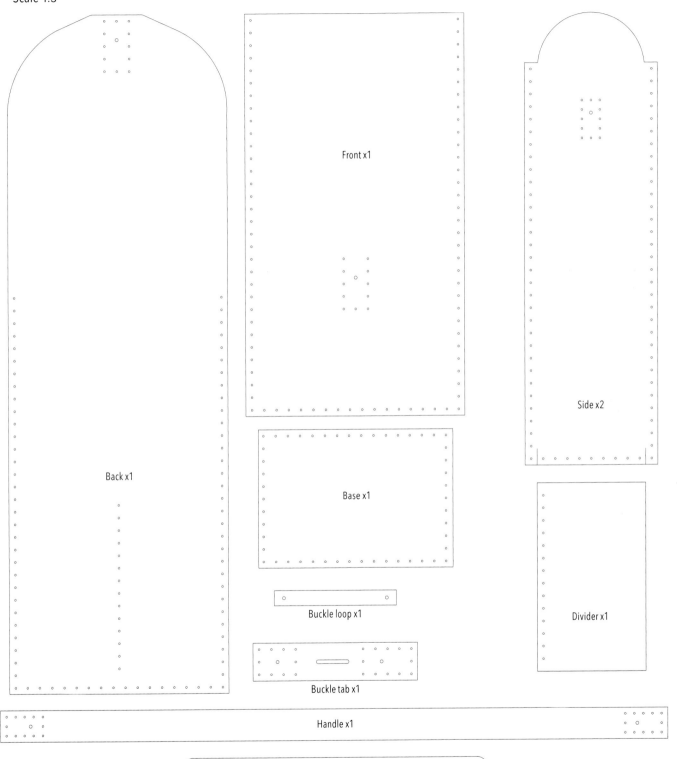

Back x1

Front x1

Base x1

Buckle loop x1

Buckle tab x1

Side x2

Divider x1

Handle x1

Closing strap x1

Adjustable BBQ apron
Scale 1:3

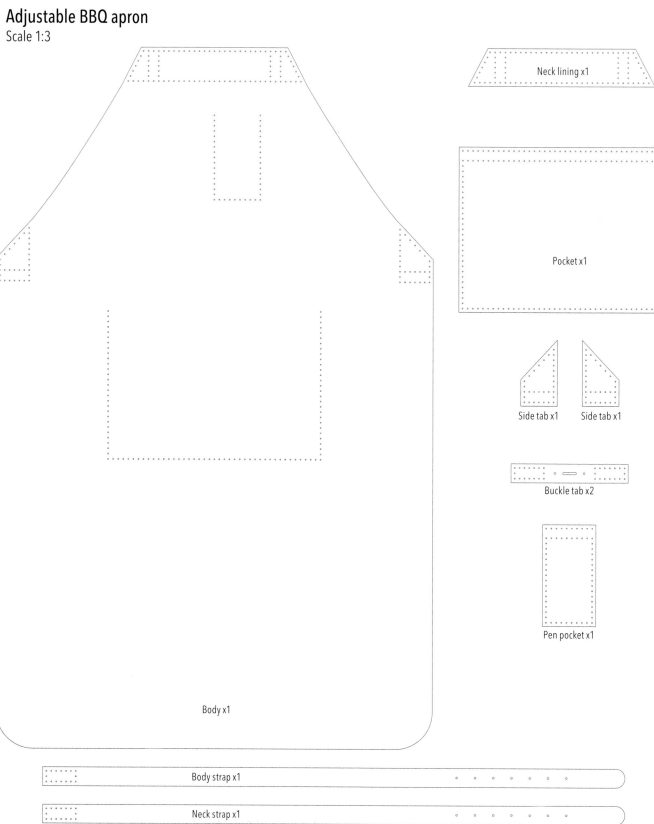

Neck lining x1

Pocket x1

Side tab x1   Side tab x1

Buckle tab x2

Pen pocket x1

Body x1

Body strap x1

Neck strap x1

Jewelry box
Scale 1:3

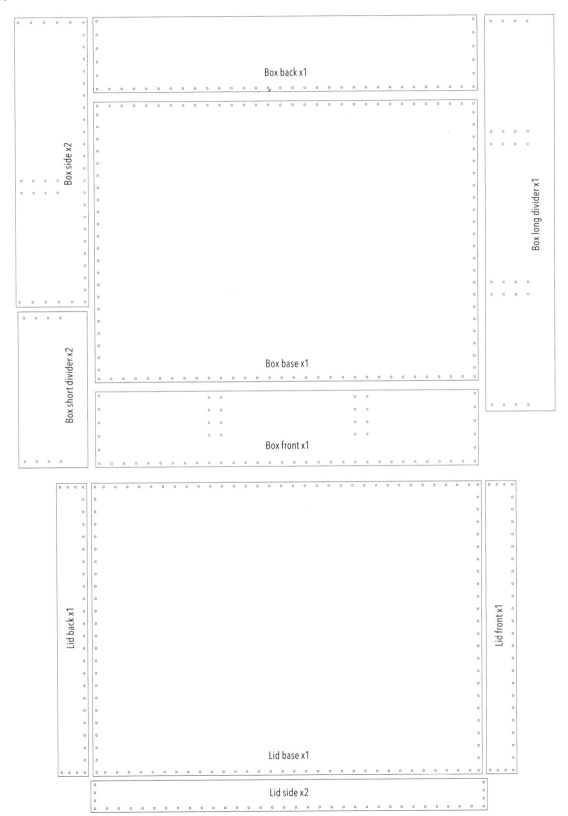

Box back x1

Box side x2

Box long divider x1

Box short divider x2

Box base x1

Box front x1

Lid back x1

Lid front x1

Lid base x1

Lid side x2

135

Photo box
Scale 1:3

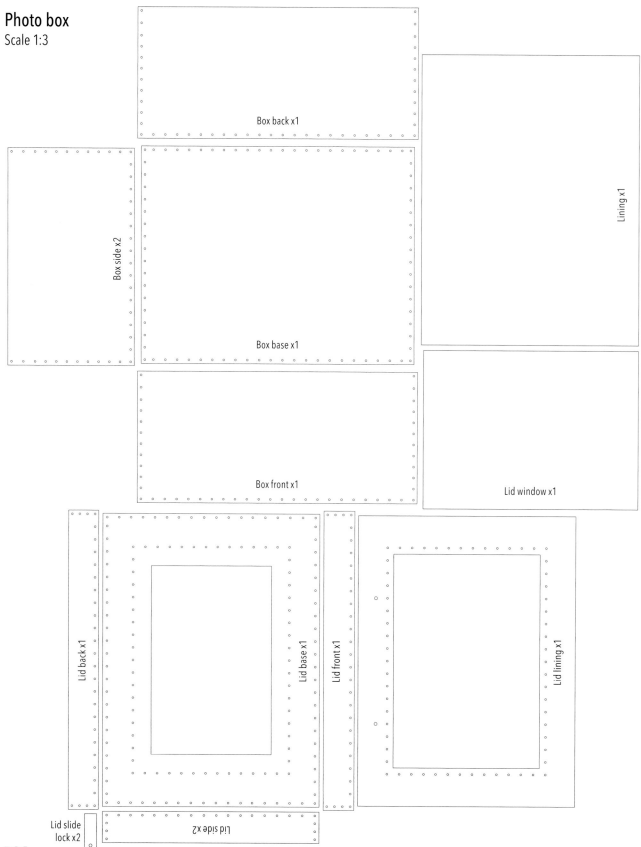

Box back x1

Lining x1

Box side x2

Box base x1

Box front x1

Lid window x1

Lid back x1

Lid base x1

Lid front x1

Lid lining x1

Lid slide
lock x2

Lid side x2

Stationery tray
Scale 1:3

Base x1

Front x1

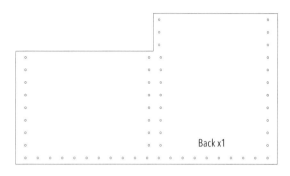

Back x1

Long divider x1

Short divider x1

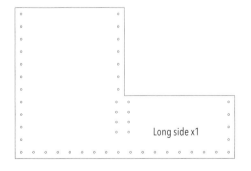

Long side x1

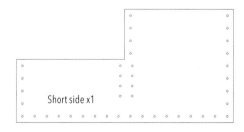

Short side x1

Hanging picture frames
Scale 1:3

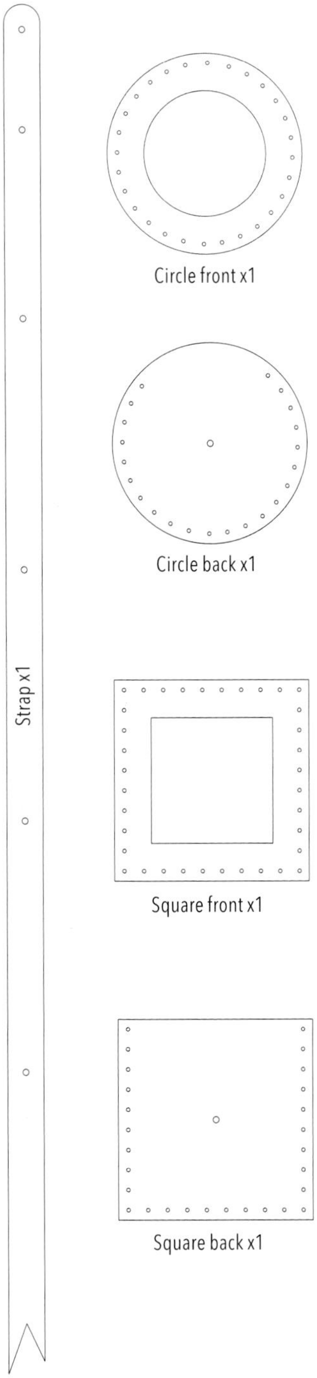

Circle front x1

Circle back x1

Square front x1

Square back x1

Strap x1

Wrist strap
Scale 1:1

Strap x1

Adjust to required length*

*Suggested final length:
Large = 250 mm (9^4/$_5$ in.)
Medium = 230 mm (9 in.)
Small = 210 mm (8^1/$_5$ in.)

Wrap-around wrist strap
Scale 1:2

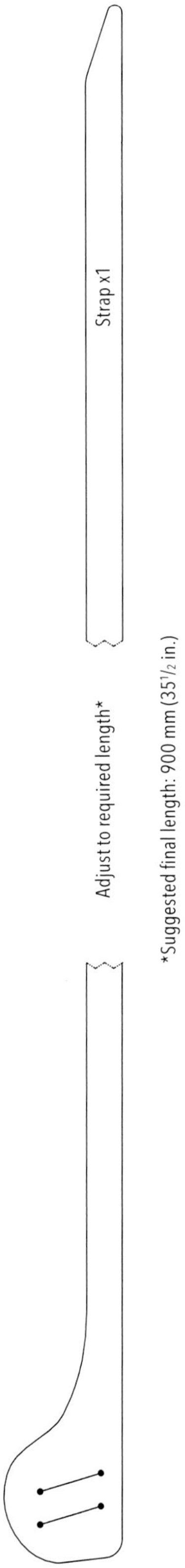

Strap x1

Adjust to required length*

*Suggested final length: 900 mm (35^1/$_2$ in.)

138

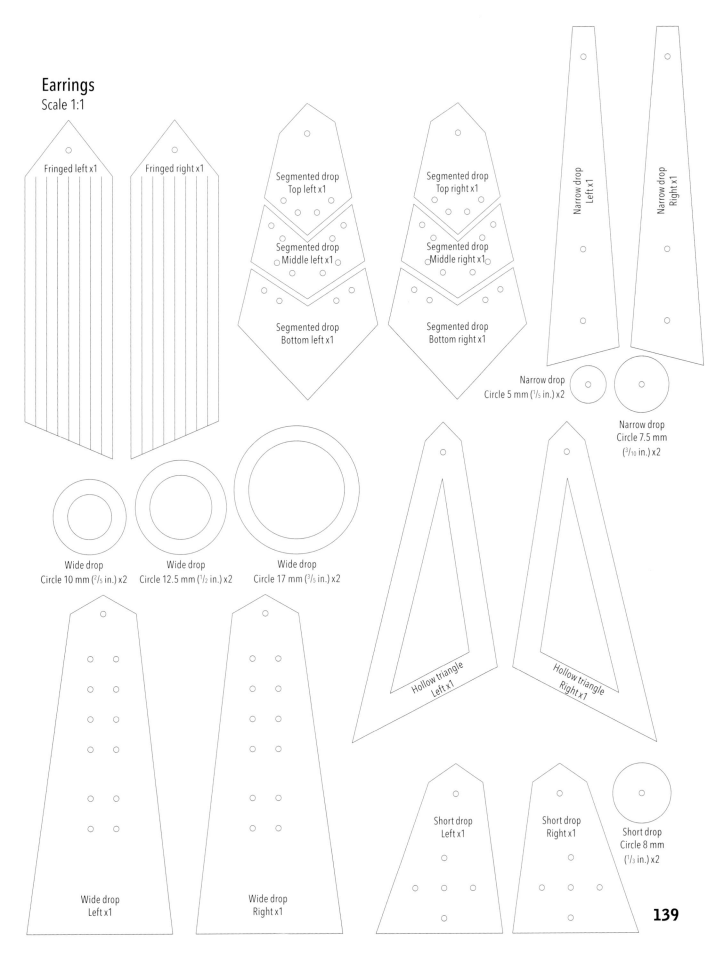

Earrings
Scale 1:1

Fringed left x1

Fringed right x1

Segmented drop
Top left x1

Segmented drop
Middle left x1

Segmented drop
Bottom left x1

Segmented drop
Top right x1

Segmented drop
Middle right x1

Segmented drop
Bottom right x1

Narrow drop
Left x1

Narrow drop
Right x1

Narrow drop
Circle 5 mm ($^1/_5$ in.) x2

Narrow drop
Circle 7.5 mm
($^3/_{10}$ in.) x2

Wide drop
Circle 10 mm ($^2/_5$ in.) x2

Wide drop
Circle 12.5 mm ($^1/_2$ in.) x2

Wide drop
Circle 17 mm ($^3/_5$ in.) x2

Hollow triangle
Left x1

Hollow triangle
Right x1

Wide drop
Left x1

Wide drop
Right x1

Short drop
Left x1

Short drop
Right x1

Short drop
Circle 8 mm
($^1/_3$ in.) x2

139

Fringed cushion cover
Scale 1:4

Back x1

Front x1

Fringing x3

Blanket roll strap

Scale 1:3

Handle x1

Handle base x1

Loop x4

Handle tab x2

Handle inner x1

Buckle tab x2

Buckle strap x1

Closing strap x2

Adjust to required length*

*Suggested final length: 875 mm (34$\frac{1}{2}$ in.)

Sling strap x1

Adjust to required length*

*Suggested final length: 1,100 mm (43$\frac{3}{10}$ in.)

Two-pocket satchel
Scale 1:4

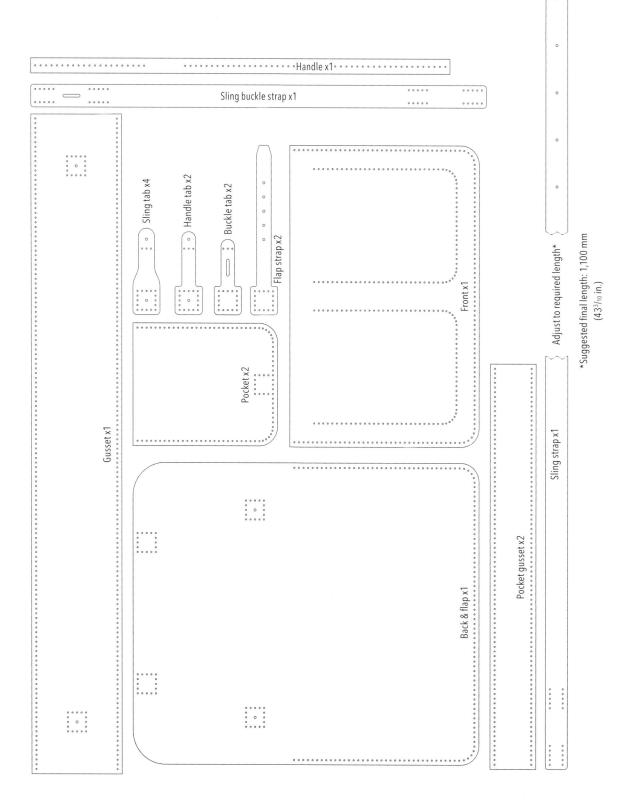

Handle x1

Sling buckle strap x1

Sling tab x4

Handle tab x2

Buckle tab x2

Flap strap x2

Front x1

Gusset x1

Pocket x2

Back & flap x1

Pocket gusset x2

Sling strap x1

Adjust to required length*

*Suggested final length: 1,100 mm
(43³/₁₀ in.)

Laptop bag
Scale 1:5

Buckle strap x1

Buckle tab x1

Loop x1

Front zipper pocket lining x1

Front x1

Back & flap x1

Gusset x1

Sling x1
Adjust to required length*

*Suggested final length: 1,290 mm (50^4/$_5$ in.)

Fringed sling bag
Scale 1:4

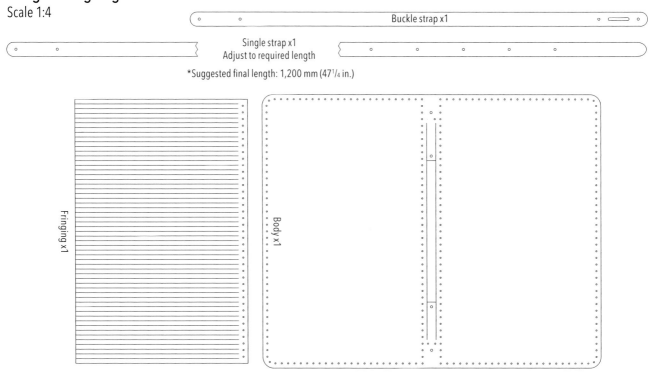

Buckle strap x1

Single strap x1
Adjust to required length

*Suggested final length: 1,200 mm (47$\frac{1}{4}$ in.)

Fringing x1

Body x1

Small sling bag
Scale 1:4

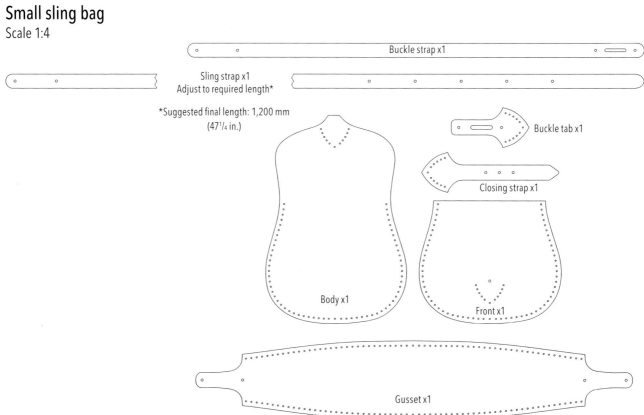

Buckle strap x1

Sling strap x1
Adjust to required length*

*Suggested final length: 1,200 mm
(47$\frac{1}{4}$ in.)

Buckle tab x1

Closing strap x1

Body x1

Front x1

Gusset x1

Basket

Scale 1:3

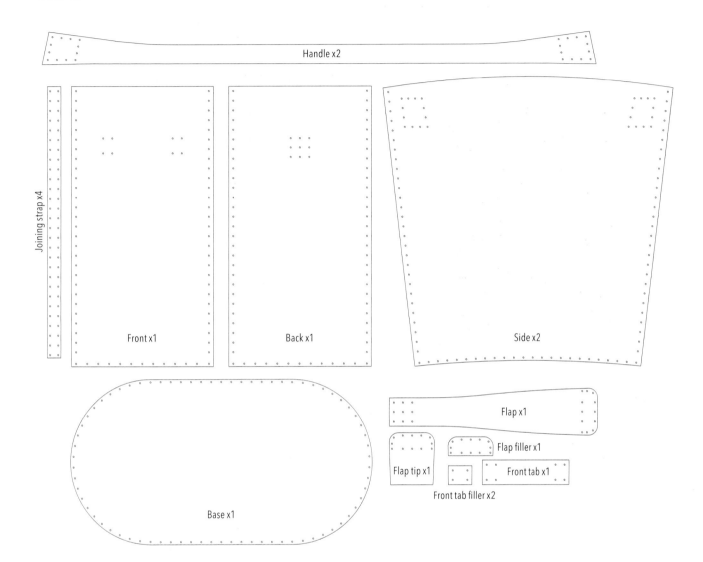

Handle x2

Joining strap x4

Front x1

Back x1

Side x2

Base x1

Flap x1

Flap filler x1

Flap tip x1

Front tab x1

Front tab filler x2

Postman's sling
Scale 1:5

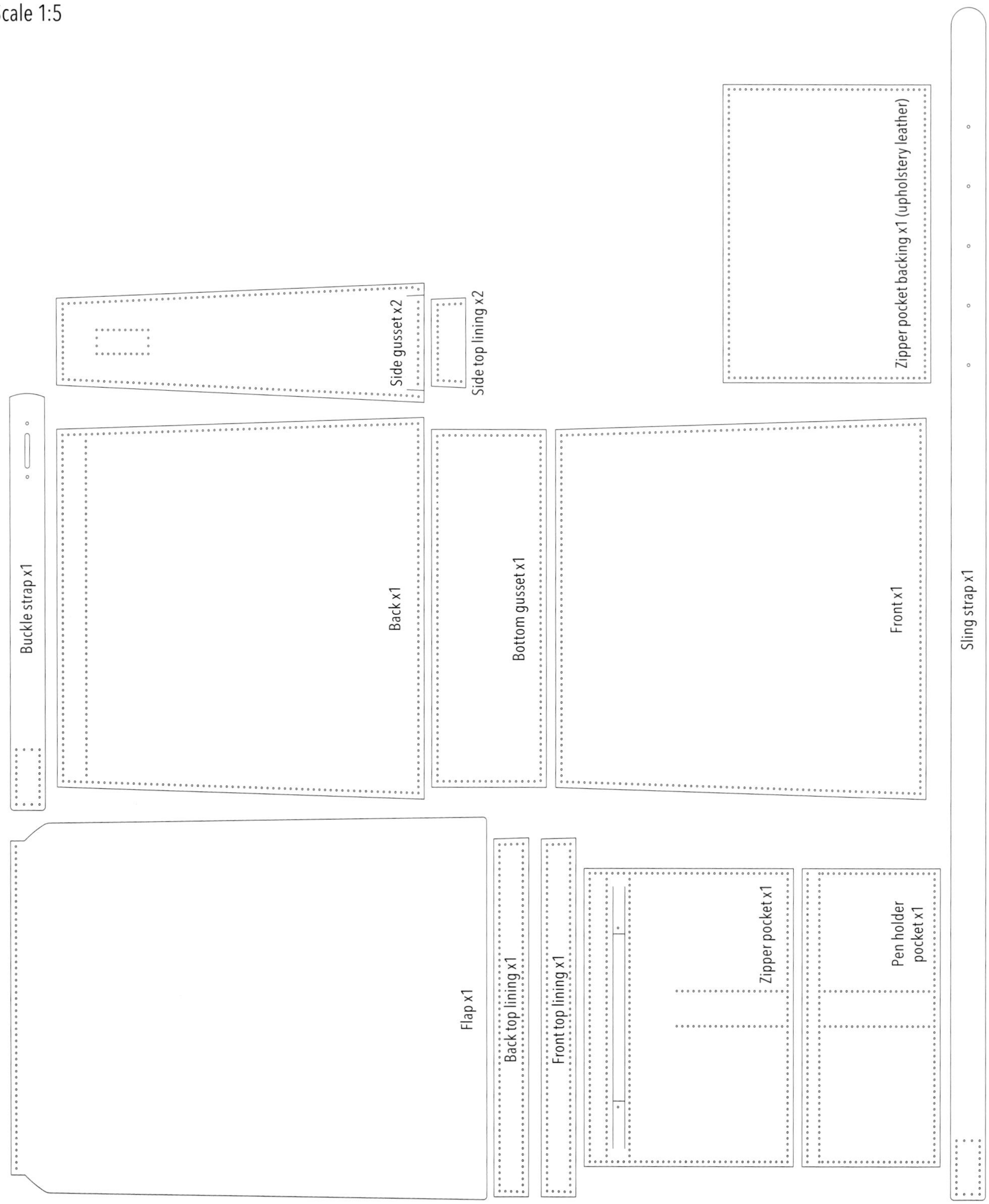

Zipper pocket backing x1 (upholstery leather)

Side gusset x2

Side top lining x2

Buckle strap x1

Back x1

Bottom gusset x1

Front x1

Sling strap x1

Flap x1

Back top lining x1

Front top lining x1

Zipper pocket x1

Pen holder pocket x1

Overnight bag
Scale 1:5

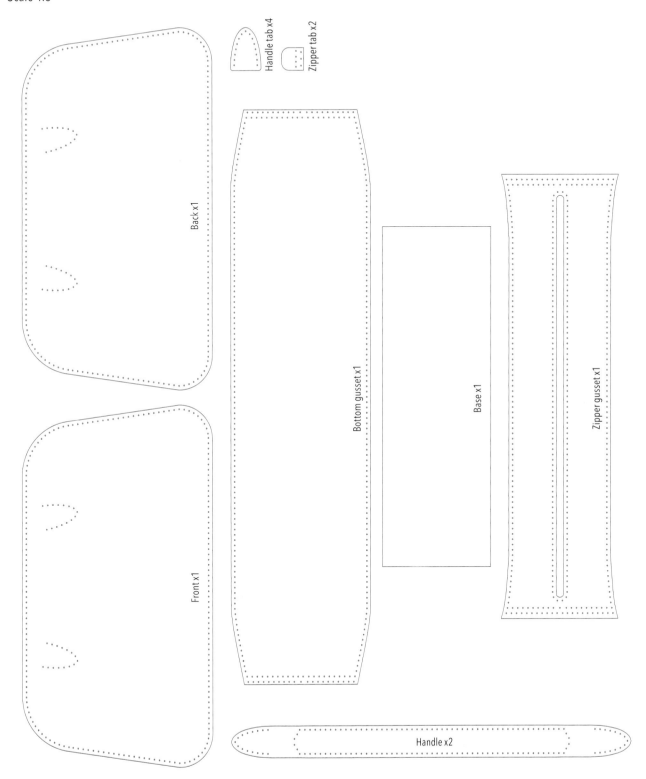

Handle tab x4

Zipper tab x2

Back x1

Bottom gusset x1

Base x1

Zipper gusset x1

Front x1

Handle x2

Studded 3-string ladies' belt
Scale 1:3

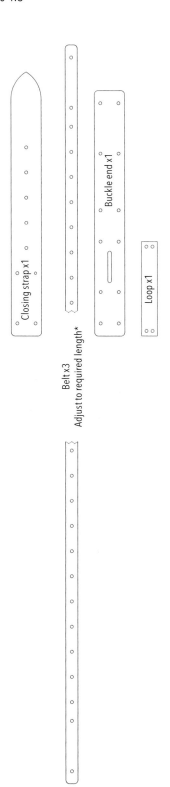

Closing strap x1

Buckle end x1

Loop x1

Belt x3
Adjust to required length*

Casual belt: 34mm
Scale 1:3

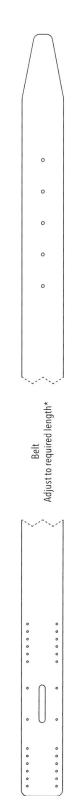

Belt
Adjust to required length*

34mm wide loop x1

Curved ladies' belt
Scale 1:5

158 x 34 mm (6$^{1}/_{5}$ x 1$^{3}/_{10}$ in.)

168 x 38 mm (6$^{3}/_{5}$ x 1$^{1}/_{2}$ in.)

178 x 41 mm (7 x 1$^{3}/_{5}$ in.)

188 x 46 mm (7$^{2}/_{5}$ x 1$^{4}/_{5}$ in.)

198 x 50 mm (7$^{4}/_{5}$ x 2 in.)

208 x 54 mm (8$^{1}/_{5}$ x 2$^{1}/_{10}$ in.)

216 x 57 mm (8$^{1}/_{2}$ x 2$^{1}/_{5}$ in.)

228 x 63 mm (9 x 2$^{1}/_{2}$ in.)

Men's wallet
Scale 1:2

Upper lining x1

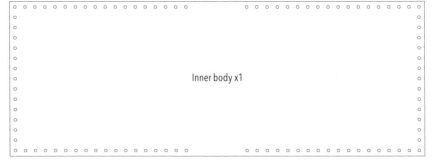

Inner body x1

Outer body x1

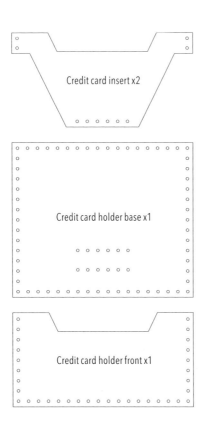

Credit card insert x2

Credit card holder base x1

Credit card holder front x1

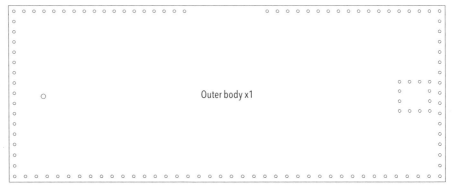

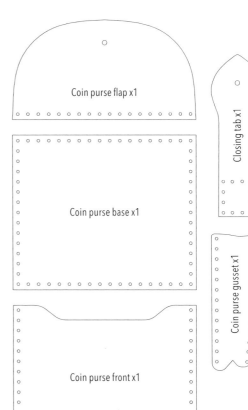

Coin purse flap x1

Closing tab x1

Coin purse base x1

Coin purse gusset x1

Coin purse front x1

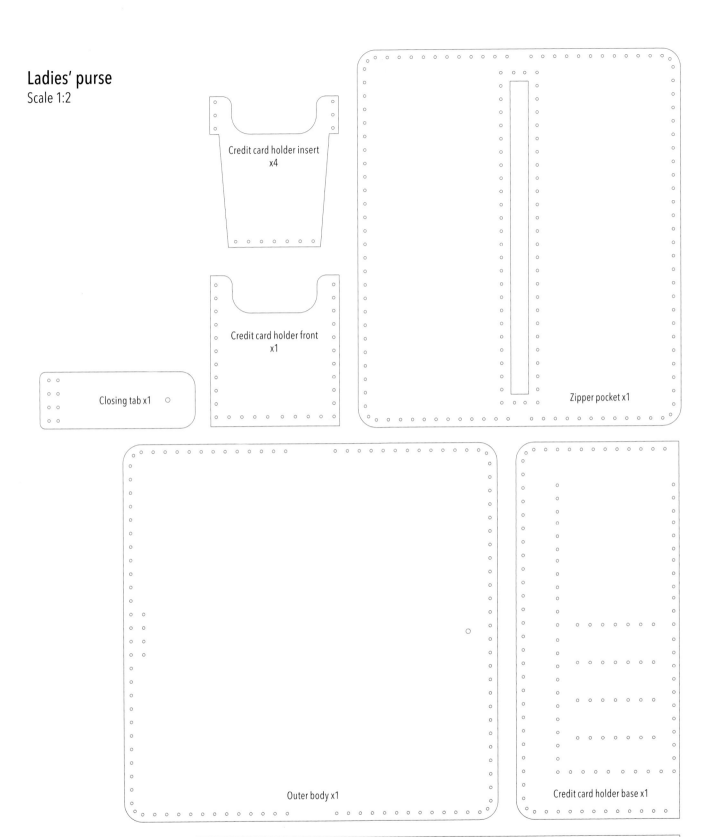

Ladies' purse
Scale 1:2

Credit card holder insert
x4

Credit card holder front
x1

Closing tab x1

Zipper pocket x1

Outer body x1

Credit card holder base x1

Gusset x1

Luggage tag
Scale 1:2

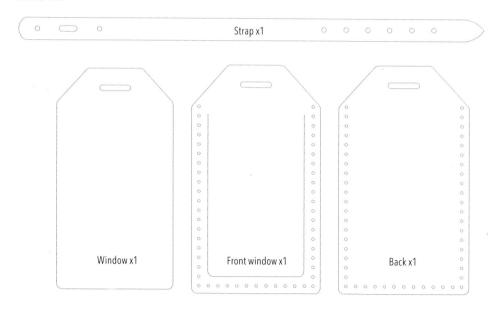

Strap x1

Window x1

Front window x1

Back x1

Coaster set
Scale 1:2

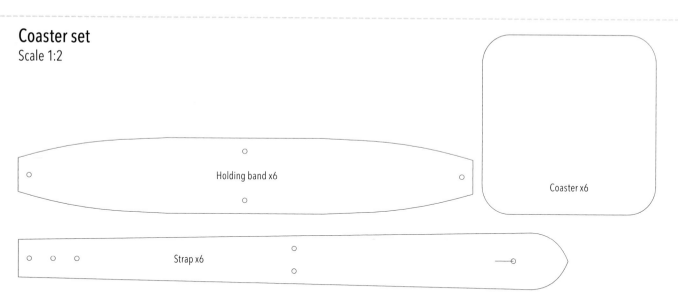

Holding band x6

Coaster x6

Strap x6

Snap hook key ring
Scale 1:2

Strap x1

Assorted key rings
Scale 1:2

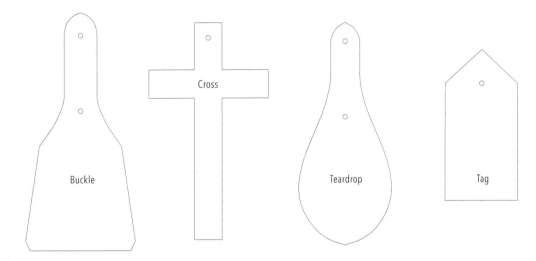

Buckle

Cross

Teardrop

Tag

Pen holder
Scale 1:2

Front x1

Back x1

Tassel key ring
Scale 1:2

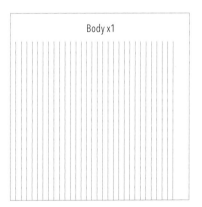

Body x1

Magic sandal: Ladies' 5¹/₂–6¹/₂
Scale 1:4

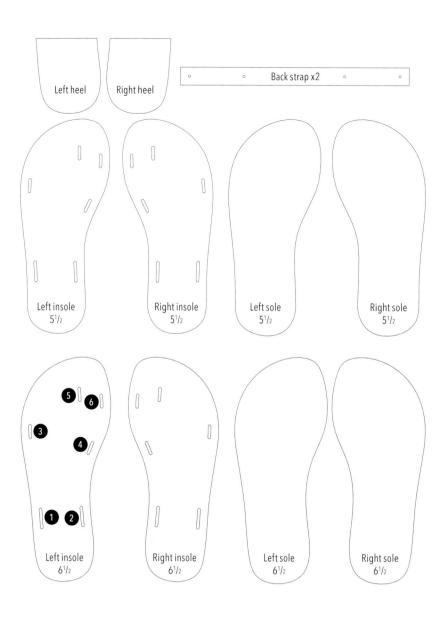

Left heel Right heel

Back strap x2

Left insole
5¹/₂

Right insole
5¹/₂

Left sole
5¹/₂

Right sole
5¹/₂

Left insole
6¹/₂

Right insole
6¹/₂

Left sole
6¹/₂

Right sole
6¹/₂

Ladies' long strap size 5¹/₂–6¹/₂ x2

Magic sandal: Ladies' 7$\frac{1}{2}$–8$\frac{1}{2}$

Scale 1:4

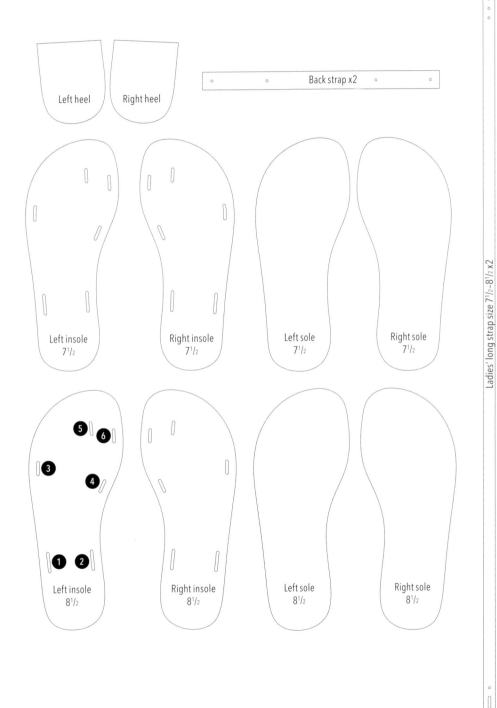

Left heel

Right heel

Back strap x2

Left insole
7$\frac{1}{2}$

Right insole
7$\frac{1}{2}$

Left sole
7$\frac{1}{2}$

Right sole
7$\frac{1}{2}$

Left insole
8$\frac{1}{2}$

Right insole
8$\frac{1}{2}$

Left sole
8$\frac{1}{2}$

Right sole
8$\frac{1}{2}$

Ladies' long strap size 7$\frac{1}{2}$–8$\frac{1}{2}$ x2

Magic sandal: Ladies' 9^1/$_2$–10^1/$_2$
Scale 1:4

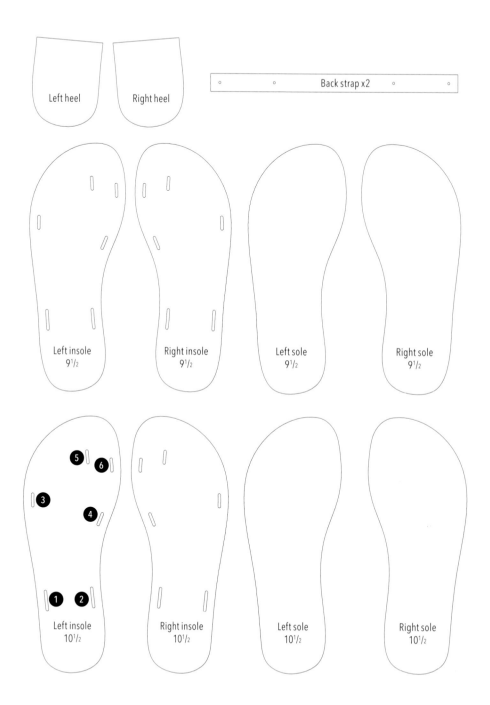

Left heel

Right heel

Back strap x2

Left insole
9^1/$_2$

Right insole
9^1/$_2$

Left sole
9^1/$_2$

Right sole
9^1/$_2$

Left insole
10^1/$_2$

Right insole
10^1/$_2$

Left sole
10^1/$_2$

Right sole
10^1/$_2$

Ladies' long strap size 9^1/$_2$–10^1/$_2$ x2

Magic sandal: Men's 6^1/$_2$–7^1/$_2$
Scale 1:4

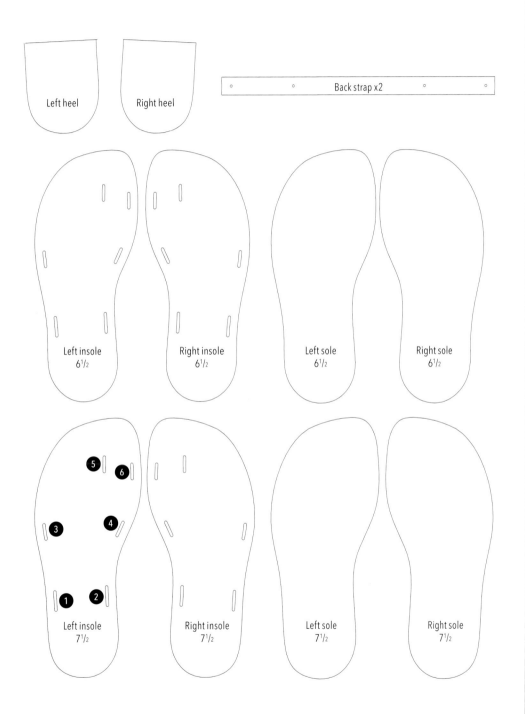

Left heel

Right heel

Back strap x2

Left insole
6^1/$_2$

Right insole
6^1/$_2$

Left sole
6^1/$_2$

Right sole
6^1/$_2$

Left insole
7^1/$_2$

Right insole
7^1/$_2$

Left sole
7^1/$_2$

Right sole
7^1/$_2$

Men's long strap size 6^1/$_2$–7^1/$_2$ x2

Magic sandal: Men's 8^1/$_2$–9^1/$_2$
Scale 1:4

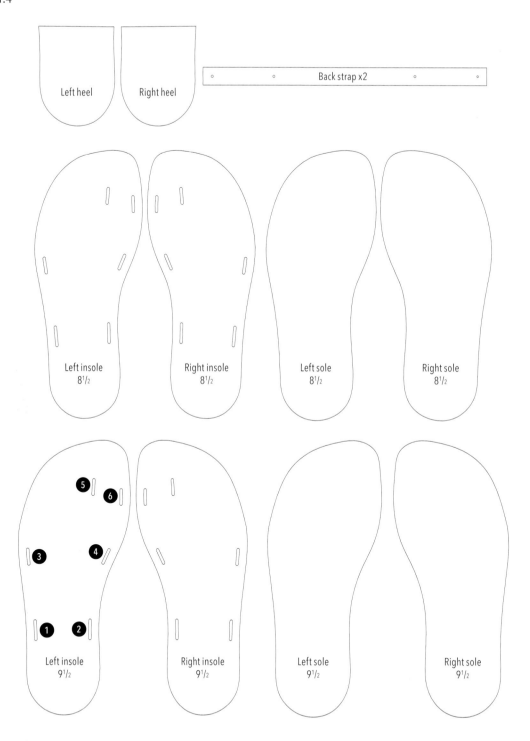

Left heel

Right heel

Back strap x2

Left insole
8^1/$_2$

Right insole
8^1/$_2$

Left sole
8^1/$_2$

Right sole
8^1/$_2$

Left insole
9^1/$_2$

Right insole
9^1/$_2$

Left sole
9^1/$_2$

Right sole
9^1/$_2$

Men's long strap size 8^1/$_2$–9^1/$_2$ x2

Magic sandal: Men's 10$^1/_2$–11$^1/_2$
Scale 1:4

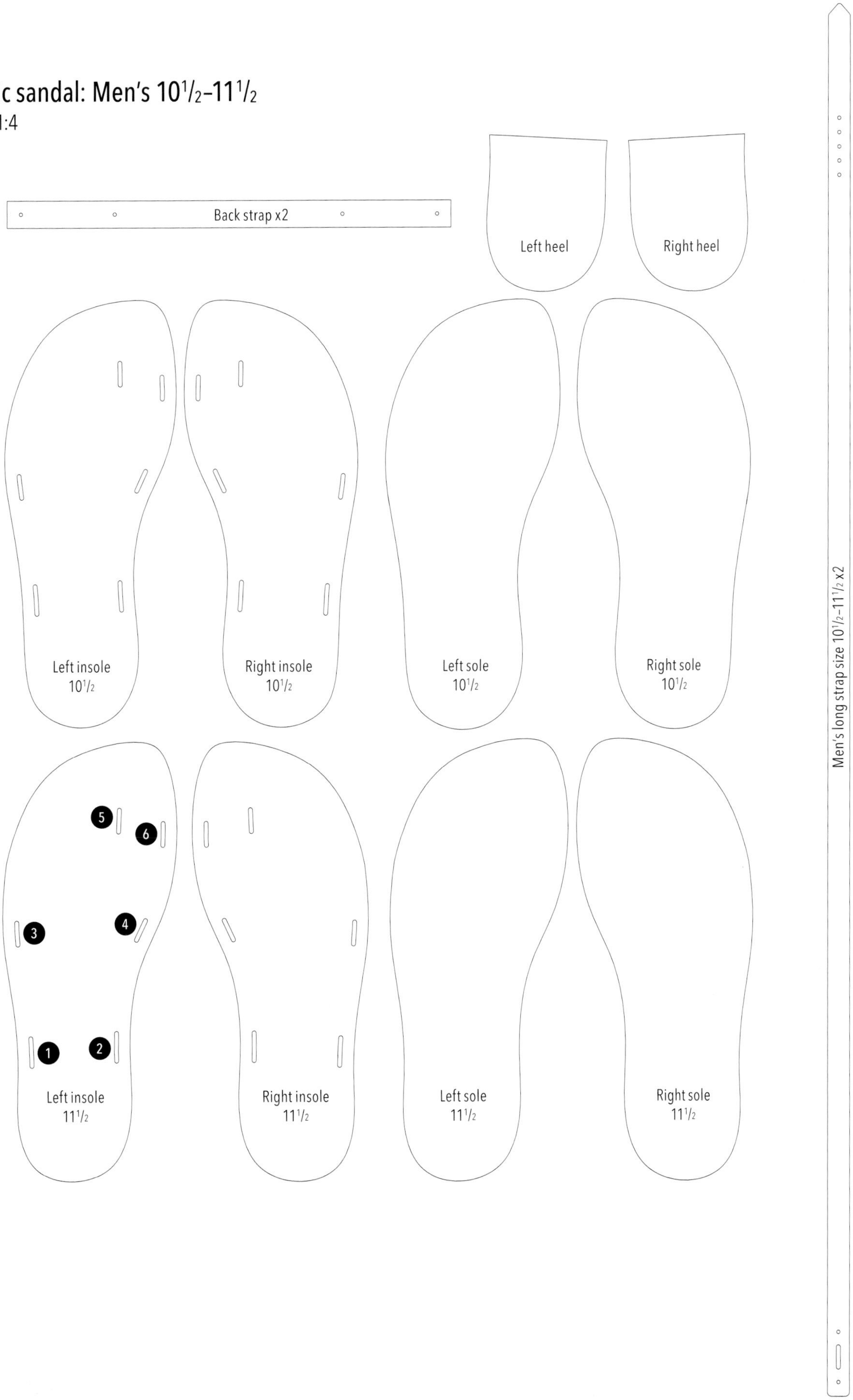

Back strap x2

Left heel

Right heel

Left insole
10$^1/_2$

Right insole
10$^1/_2$

Left sole
10$^1/_2$

Right sole
10$^1/_2$

Left insole
11$^1/_2$

Right insole
11$^1/_2$

Left sole
11$^1/_2$

Right sole
11$^1/_2$

Men's long strap size 10$^1/_2$–11$^1/_2$ x2

159

Pouffe
Scale 1:5

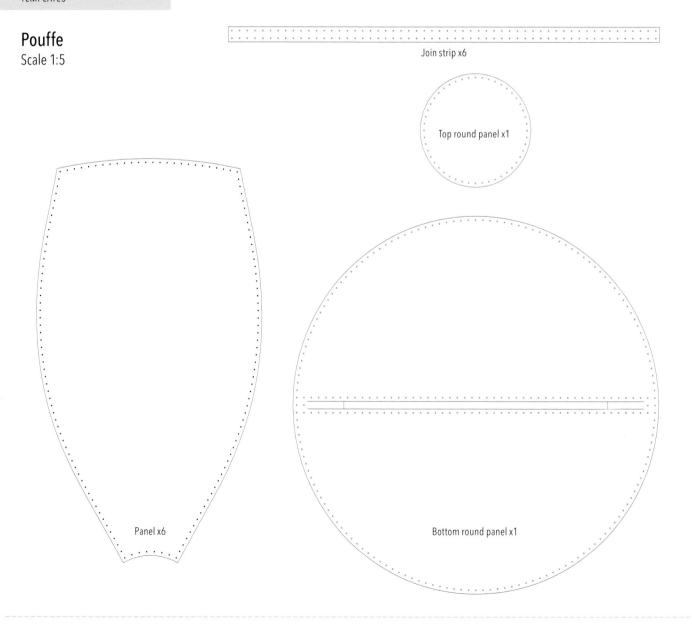

Join strip x6

Top round panel x1

Panel x6

Bottom round panel x1

Business-card holder
Scale 1:2

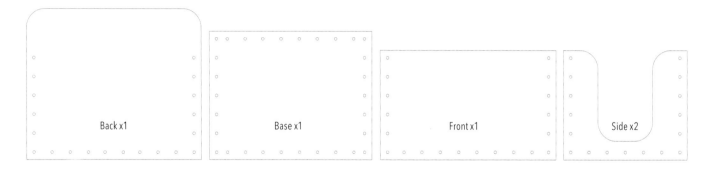

Back x1

Base x1

Front x1

Side x2